GO LEFT!

By

Bill Hogan

ISBN 978-1-105-53054-8

CONTENTS

PREFACE

GO LEFT is 180° from traditional selling techniques; in fact, none of those techniques, including "closing" are part of our program. Rather, three fundamental principles – all based entirely on human psychology are presented and fully explained:

- The first principle is total FOCUS on the PROSPECT rather than oneself.
- The second is total INVOLVEMENT or having prospects get "skin in the game."
- The third principal is DISCOVERY; that is, prospects discover for themselves whether their problems are serious enough to change, and if so, exactly what those changes (solution) should be.

"GET REAL" is the overriding theme of the book. In other words, salespeople should understand exactly where they stand at any time during the sales process – is the business imminent, in the future, or ever? To that end three key rules are explored:

- No Pain…No Change.
- The primary job of a salesperson is to get a decision, and "No" and "No for now" are decisions.
- Be the winner or the first one out.

Our sales training programs promote Repetition and Reinforcement. In fact, it's been said that people need to hear a new concept up to six times before he/she begins to implement it. To that end, several principles written in this book have been purposely repeated.

ACKNOWLEDGEMENTS

Many thanks to the thousands of salespeople, sales managers, owners, clients and prospects whose interactions over the past 20 years have profoundly influenced the development of this book.

Special thanks to the late David Sandler, David Kurlan, Al Strauss and Bill Bonnstetter for their sales mentorship.

"NO! I CAN'T BE BOTHERED TO DO ANY TRAINING – WE'VE GOT A BATTLE TO FIGHT"

INTRODUCTION

STORY:

In 2004, our company, Hogan Leadership Group, was hired to conduct a sales training program for a midsize service company. The leader in their business (a Fortune 10 company) was so dominant that their annual sales was three times that of the nearest competitor. Our company was in the middle of the pack of those competitors.

A newly promoted vice president of sales and marketing who had just hired us was charged with setting the strategic direction for the company. After several months of group planning, the VP and senior management made a critical decision. Rather than going head to head with the industry leader, they decided to target one specific user group.

This strategy turned out to be genius.

However, a funny thing happened on the way to success—implementation. The VP had indeed planned all the *services* that must go along with the user group. Also, in hiring us, he was convinced that our unique sales process was all that was needed. Not so!

By accident and good luck (see footnote to story on p. 17), the VP realized that our program of **"Involvement"**—*getting the prospect involved*—also had to be integrated within his own company. He then began to institute a company-wide sales culture, that is, any and all departments that had anything to do with sales had to become familiar with our sales program. And they had to support it, large and small, within each department's respective expertise. In essence, each department was saying to sales, "How can we help?"

Footnote:

1. At the end of 2010 not only was this company clearly number two in the industry, but they were also closing in on the leader.

2. The company now dominates this specific user group.

3. The most striking result, however, was that they accomplished this with *fewer* sales people! That's right. In seven years, the company doubled their business with 20% fewer sales people! From this sales budget savings, they hired support personnel and instituted programs and services that made it not only difficult but also expensive for competitors to duplicate.

Takeaways:

1. Many companies mistake their emphasis on customer service as evidence of a company-wide sales culture. It is only a piece of the pie. For one, all of the "silos"—that is, individual disciplines and services of a company—must communicate and interact directly or indirectly with the sales department.

2. Also, developing a company strategy that can be easily copied will ultimately prove ineffective. Our client made their strategy difficult if not impossible to duplicate, beginning with a "focus on the prospect" process with total involvement.

3. The three-prong attack proved to be the ultimate strategy for reaching the company's growth goals:

    - Develop and focus on a target market
    - Establish a sales culture—entire company should become customer focused
    - Implement a totally different sales process.

We strongly believe that these three principles share equal importance to business growth, and, to that end, we have devoted Chapter 8 to the first two strategies. For further detailed information, we suggest the book *On Your Mark...Get Set...Grow!* by Tom Donato.

However, number three—implement a totally different sales process—is what *Go Left* is all about.

When attempting to secure new business, the typical challenges salespeople face include:

1. Prospects' general lack of trust in salespeople.

2. Prospects primarily looking for free information, including costs, while offering minimum information themselves.

3. Prospects remaining in control of the sales process.

However, the real culprit is *change.* You know the popular saying, "I'm all for change as long as it's you who changes not me!" Only *20%* of the population willingly changes. The overwhelming majority only change when forced to do so.

Creating change, therefore, is the heart and soul of *Going Left*. Its *purpose* is to help prospects identify key issues that would encourage/enable them to change. The *process* initially gets prospects talking and ultimately has them commit to working together with the salesperson. In addition, as the issues are developed, the aforementioned three challenges quickly begin to melt away.

This book is designed to be a concise yet thorough how-to book involving a complete selling process. It is hands-on and to the point—just the way salespeople like it!

Go Left includes seven specific steps that make a sale and likewise the subtle shortfalls that can break it. In addition, the roadmap for successful sales that makes up Chapter 7 is a must for *sales managers*, and the advice given in Chapter 8, hopefully, will demonstrate to corporate executives the critical importance of maximizing resources company-wide.

However, no book on selling will in itself magically—*abracadabra!*—improve your selling skills any more than reading a book about swimming will make you a swimmer. How many non swimmers would jump in the ocean immediately after reading such a book?

Therefore, the best use of this book is as a ready reference. For best results, we recommend that you use a highlighter during the first read and continually reread the specific chapter/section that refers to your current situation.

Go Left focuses on the totally different sales process that our clients implement, the one which we term "Go Left." The treatment is direct, a learn how-to manual that has plenty of meat on the bone. No reader will go away unnourished. *Go Left* shows how to create customer involvement in the sales process. It rewards those who master the art of listening and presents a unique, seemingly counterintuitive approach to making quality sales. *Go Left* shows by example and direction how to build trust, how to build a sale, and how to build a business. *Go Left* is for all those who want to learn how to better secure new business, especially in the hard-to-crack mature markets that make up today's business environment, with a proven method of selling.

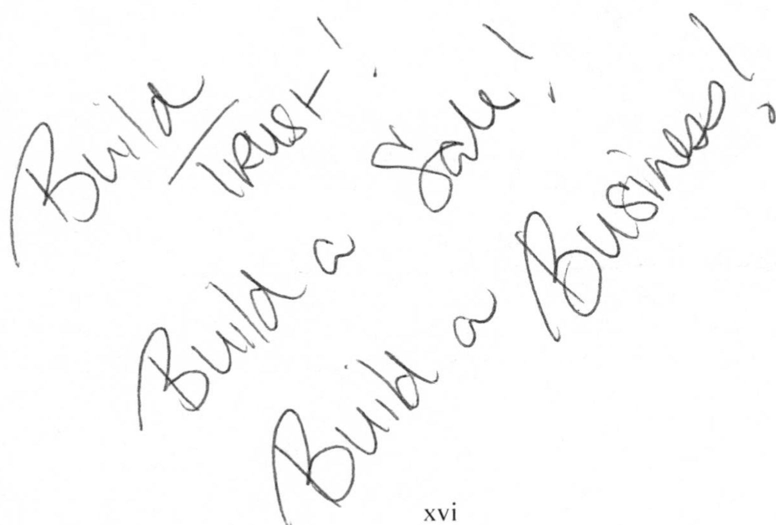

Chapter 1

Dysfunctional Selling: Take the Cure

Feature/Benefit=Me Too Marketing

Several years ago, we were conducting a sales training program for new salespeople when the vice president of sales stopped in to observe. It was early in the program and the class was discussing the effects and results of featúre/benefit selling.

The VP listened a while and then joined the discussion. On the table were several company brochures—his along with his competitors. He reached for his company's brochure and raised it for all to see.

"Take a look at this brochure and compare it to the brochures of our main competitors. If you were to cut the tops off of every one of them, so you could not read the company names, not one of us could correctly identify any of the companies. The brochures are all the same. They're all filled with features and benefits—they're nearly 100% identical!"

What he left unsaid was that feature/benefit selling by way of company brochures really says, "Me too." It leaves the prospect with little if any understanding of the difference between you and your competitors. This is compounded when prospects, who routinely attempt to commoditize your product or service, discern nothing unique about you and your company's offerings when reading these brochures. In other words, while you are trying to prove that you are different and that your services or products are unique, prospects, too, often believe, "They're all alike." Result? You've literally forced the prospect to make a decision based solely on price.

Asking Questions is a First Step—Go Left, Complete the Journey

"Now, wait a minute," you say. "I just don't give feature/benefit presentations. First, I ask questions to uncover a prospect's specific or unique needs and then—and only then—do I explain our product/service and how it will help (the benefit) them."

Well, this is a good start…but it's only a start. There are three considerations that determine the effectiveness of any question and answer sessions with a prospect.

The ***first*** is that you, as the sales person, must accept everything that the prospect says as the truth. At this early stage of the relationship, there is little ancillary information concerning the prospect's needs that would allow you to doubt the prospect or identify a contradiction. You're following as much as leading…and always believing that the prospect's perception is reality.

Secondly, you have no way of determining whether the situation facing the prospect is serious enough for him/her to make a change. You have to assume that change—more specifically, the resistance to change—will not be an obstacle in the way of a purchase.

And ***third***, the early rounds of the question and answer sessions between the seller and the buyer are usually slow in developing the conditions and opportunities for the prospect to ***discover*** the solution. In the ***Go Left*** approach, you want the ***buyer*** to realize that your product or service is the solution to his/her problem. When the prospect takes this initiative, he/she will have an emotional attachment to the solution. It's his baby and he's proud of it. Remember, people buy with emotion first, and then reinforce the purchasing decision with logic or rational argument.

Formula for Failure: F/B +/- PP = Commodity

Feature/benefit selling and premature proposals (a product or service proposed to a prospect without ascertaining the prospect's special needs) are the primary ingredients of the dysfunctional selling system. Employing either one or both simply encourages the prospect to consider your product/service a commodity; thus, making a decision based solely on price.

Thus, dysfunctional selling can be memorialized with this simple formula: a F/B (feature/benefit) presentation with *or* without a PP (premature proposal) results in your product/service being perceived as a *commodity*.

Unfortunately, most, if not all, selling systems today are based on this formula. Cloned brochures are not the only example. Another example: a typical first face-to-face meeting with a prospective new client begins with a salesperson asking "qualifying questions." The first qualifier is often this: "Does the prospect have enough need or interest in hearing about the salesperson's product/service?" A simple "yes" and the dysfunctional selling system is off and running!

What is Driving Feature/Benefit Selling?

Two main factors:

1. *The prospect is looking for free information about the salesperson's product/service including pricing.* In his quest, he will always offer enough generalities for the salesperson to continue, such as "we're thinking about changing vendors" or "we're not happy with the service provided by our current vendor" or "our sales representative does not contact us often enough." These are usually enough to pry loose the information and not incidentally torpedo the sale.
2. *Salespeople are trained to give feature/benefit presentations.* In fact, very often, salespeople get more satisfaction from a great presentation than from getting the sale. Wrong way to go. The salesperson is not "Going Left." He's going home—without the sale, without any progress toward a sale, without any in-depth knowledge of the client, including the all-important special needs that may match what the salesperson's company can offer.

Such a meeting usually ends with a perfunctory good-bye: "Thank you, this is just what we need; we'll get back to you." Dysfunction continues because the prospect has or at least believes that he has all the information he needs. He is now in complete control of the rest of the sales process. The salesperson is at the mercy of the prospect and often falls into "follow-up limbo" marked by calls that are rarely returned.

There are times, of course, when the prospect does, in fact, reach out again to the salesperson, usually asking for a proposal. Again dysfunction is perpetuated because the salesperson either has limited information to customize a proposal or has been given specifications to bid along with at least two other competitors. In this scenario, if the prospect does make a change, it is almost always based on price.

It Gets Worse

If price is the sole determinant for a prospect making a buy, there will be fewer quality sales, fewer loyal clients, and less loyalty in general. Here is a litany of killer complaints that result from feature/benefit presentations.
Read 'em and weep:

5 KILLER COMPLAINTS

1. I try to build rapport and eagerly give outstanding presentations only to get a "think-it-over" and ultimately fall into "follow-up limbo" (calls aren't returned).

2. I deliver detailed proposals only to have them shopped.

3. I feel passionate about my product/service and have a genuine interest in helping prospects solve their problems, yet they insist on three bids.

4. When I lose business, I usually get, "Your price was too high."

5. Even when my price is lower, I still do not get the business because the prospect shows it to h/h current provider who matches my price and/or value offering.

In examining these sales phenomena, doesn't it seem one-sided? The salesperson tries his best to help his prospects, and yet not only does he not get the business but he also is even more frustrated because he feels he's been used. Before we start making corrections or improvements, let's look into how this feature/benefit sales technique got started and why this continues to occur today.

HISTORY: Why Do So Many Bad Things Happen to Good People?

In the early 1950s, Xerox literally exploded on the scene with the world's finest paper copier. Leesburg, Virginia became its main training center, and Xerox soon became acknowledged as the "Father of Sales Training." The above is well documented. What isn't generally known, however, is what department within Xerox was responsible. Hint: it wasn't sales or marketing; rather it was the *purchasing* department. That's right, purchasing! The rationale? In prior years, salesmen (yes, salesmen; there were no saleswomen in those days) simply called on purchasing agents and "presented" their wares.

As Xerox grew, purchasing agents were being bombarded with salesmen whose products and services were of no use. Therefore, purchasing agents began to demand that salesmen ask "qualifying questions" first. If and only if the prospect (Xerox) answered positively could the salesman present or demonstrate his product/service. Made good sense! And thus was the birth of "qualify and present." Presentation became known as "feature/benefit presentations—explaining a product's/service's features and how each can benefit the prospect.

Soon after, IBM began to teach its salesmen the same "qualify and present" process. So here, you have two of the largest sales forces in the country using this process. The two companies continued to grow, constantly ranking among the largest and most successful companies in the USA if not the world. Xerox seized the opportunity to market its sales training program, and, not surprisingly, had instant success. Most companies flocked to the training. (How could you argue with success?) And sales training, as we know it today, was launched!

Both these companies had market shares in the 90th percentile. Question: if you worked for a company with 90% market share, would you even be reading this book? How much sales training would anyone need if they had little or no competition?

The purchasing department developed this process with the added benefit of keeping total *control* of the sales process. Other training companies jumped on the bandwagon. But down through the years, while virtually the entire world changed, sales training changed very little.

Trust (Or Lack of Trust) Is an Issue

Even though the sales process favored the prospect, there was very little effect on the ultimate outcome of a sale, primarily due to overall trust. At that time, we lived in a very trusting society. In fact, trust in general was so high that in many neighborhoods people never even locked their doors!

The big change came about during the Vietnam War. How? It was the first time in modern history that our government was seriously challenged by the general population. But first, let's go back *before* the war. (You may need your parents or grandparents for help here.) On a scale of 1–10, with "10" being the highest, rate the trust factor for each of the following: our government, the police, teachers, and the clergy. Didn't most of you rate each fairly high? Now, let's go through the same group today…very different numbers, right?

Finally, let's add one more group to the mix—salespeople. Where are we in the food chain? Not very high. Let's be honest, pretty low, right? How many parents brag that their son or daughter is a salesperson? In fact, we don't even like to admit it ourselves! You say we're wrong? Look at your business card and tell us how many say Salesperson or Sales Representative vs. Marketing Specialist, New Business Developer, Territory Manager, Product/Project Manager…etc.

Now, if lack of trust is the issue, what is the result of this problem? Good question! First, let me ask: if you have an innate mistrust of a group and then have a one-on-one conversation with a member of that group, how open and honest are you going to be? Not very much, right? So much then for "qualifying questions" in traditional selling. Sure, you can ask all the right questions, but how do you know you're getting the right answers? You don't, and rarely do you get the whole truth. For example, you get a call from a prospect: "We'd like to see you, we're thinking very seriously of using your product/service. In fact, we'd like to get a proposal as soon as possible." Translation: "We want your number so we can check it against our current supplier and perhaps get an even better price from him. Can you identify with this situation?

Why do so many companies insist on "getting three bids"? Because they just can't wait to read all about your product/service, right? Unless you still believe in the tooth fairy, you know they only look at the back page with cost figures.

Lack of Trust Feeds Buyers' Fears

This lack of trust leads to fears and negative assumptions concerning the salesperson and/or the sales process, some of which include:

1. *Fear of buyers' remorse*

   Buyers are afraid that even though buying from you today looks like the thing to do, they'll regret that decision tomorrow, next week, or next month. This fear increases in direct proportion to the price and the number of choices they must pick from.

2. *Fear that the wrong choice will diminish respect and esteem from others*

   Peer pressure does not lose impact once we leave our teens. We continue for the approval and recognition of our peers. This fear increases if the buyer has strong social needs, serves a domineering boss, works in a team environment, or is employed by a company demanding continuous improvement and excellence.

3. *Fear of the unknown*

   Regardless of assurances and guarantees from you, buyers may be more content to stick to a *painful* status quo than to opt for an uncertain future. They may not like what they currently have, but they know what they currently have. (The devil you know is better than the devil you don't know.) The future is too big a question mark to take any risks. This fear is especially pronounced for buyers whose job may not be assured and for those who lack self-confidence.

4. *Fear of relinquishing control to you*

Like all people, buyers want to feel in control. They want to call the shots, establish an agenda, and keep the upper hand. They are comforted by the power of being able to delay purchase decisions as long as they want. Once you interfere with that control, you reduce their power and elevate their fears.

Furthermore, this lack of trust also promotes negative assumptions:

1. *Buyers believe it's OK to get free consulting from you.*

They see nothing wrong with using your expertise to help them make a good decision with your competitors. After all, you called them; they didn't call you. And you're on their territory, not vice versa.

2. *Buyers believe their time is more valuable than your time.*

3. *Buyers believe that stalling and delaying are right and necessary.*

They believe that the more they control in the negotiation the greater their psychological security. Their ultimate control is deciding whether or not to place the order. The longer they delay that decision, the greater their own sense of security.

4. *Buyers believe that even though you may look like a nice person, your job forces you to compromise your ethics and integrity.*

STUDIES: *If prospects do not trust salespeople, then what are they looking for in a quality salesperson?*

Over the years, there have been many studies conducted that show the disconnect between prospect expectations and the sales process. One of the most significant research studies was conducted by the Chally Group, a nationally known consulting company, which surveyed prospects to determine what they were looking for (salespeople to focus on the prospect's problems and solutions).

Conducted over ten years, the survey included 24,000 *decision makers* who were asked to define ***world-class excellence***, what they'd like in a quality sales person, and how they conduct business. Here is what they found.

1. Customers are substantially more concerned with the *effectiveness* of the salesperson than they are with the solutions being offered.
2. They would like salespeople to provide customer advocacy; that is, partnership development.
3. The goal should be a high-quality decision based on value (a signed order cannot be the ultimate goal in a true partnership).
4. The price of the solution ranked dead last in the top criteria.

<u>Summary</u>

- It does not make economic, ethical, logical, or any other sense to present a solution, if the *incentive to change* has not been established.
- *Diagnosis and agreement with the diagnosis between the parties,* the buyer and the seller (not the seller's presentation), form the proper basis for an ensuing sale.

In order to get perspective from the *sellers* point of view, Microsoft conducted a live meeting webinar several years ago, which included 400 salespeople.

Results:

1. 90% of the content of their presentations and proposals *focused on their own companies*, while only 10% focused on customer problems and the customer world.
2. The overwhelming emphasis was on solution features and benefits; however, the customer was left to connect the dots.
3. Only 22% of customers had high quality decision processes in place.

Harvard Business School, in reviewing this report concluded: "Solution sellers continue to outrun the *comprehension and requirements* of the customer."

So how are you feeling right now? Let's review:

1. Traditional sales processes allow prospects to remain in total control.
2. Prospects minimally trust salespeople.
3. While salespeople attempt to sell value, prospects try to make the product/service a commodity (i.e., price driven).
4. Most often, prospects stay with their current vendor.

Against these odds, what chance do salespeople really have? Many if not most simply resort to the numbers game—you know, throw enough stuff against the wall and hope enough sticks. Doesn't sound like a really fulfilling career, does it? Not likely to produce a solid ROI for anyone else either.

Before you throw in the towel, let's think about the *real* problem. It's not prospects and it's not salespeople; the real culprit is the sales process that remains totally dysfunctional. Go to your local bookstore—the business section—and see how few books are there on selling. Why? Because in the past 60 years, there has been no real change to the sales process! Oh, some sophistication and increased professionalism has been added—"qualify and present" became "need satisfaction selling," became "solution selling," became "relationship selling," became whatever the book of the season called it. However, the guts of every training program today still revolve around:

1. Qualifying questions—assuming honest answers
2. Offering solutions—with limited prospect information
3. Answering objections—without discovering the real problem(s)
4. Closing—using techniques often considered manipulative

Remember also that while the sales process has changed little, *purchasing* techniques have changed dramatically.

So let's discuss a **realistic sales process**—one that speaks to the decision maker's desire for a high quality decision based on value. Are people more apt to accept an idea they perceive as their own or an idea they perceive as someone else's? You're absolutely right. The overwhelming majority is more apt to accept an idea that they perceive as their own**.** However, current selling systems involve *convincing* prospects as opposed to *discovery*—helping them discover the solution or ***Going Left***.

Do people buy emotionally or intellectually? They buy emotionally and then reinforce their decisions intellectually. Once again most selling systems appeal to the intellectual side, while ***Going Left*** appeals to the emotional side. Therefore, ***Going Left*** is a sales process that is *exactly opposite* to traditional dysfunctional processes. It is discussed in detail in the following chapters.

- Discovery vs. Convincing
- Appealing to one's Emotions vs. their Intellect
- Involvement vs. Arm's-Length Relationship
- Getting Real—does prospect have a real need or just price shopping?

You're now at decision time. If you are a salesperson, are you willing to make a complete change and start ***Going Left***? If you are in sales support, marketing, or a product expert, are you prepared to make the leap from feature/benefit presentations to ones that are customer focused?

If you are senior management, are you willing to support a sales process that does not give the comfort of measuring sales activity in the traditional sense, such as number of proposals?

Don't answer too quickly—take an honest look at yourself. Remember, *80%* of the population does not like change. Are you in the *80%* or the *20%*? I cannot help but mention a little irony here. In securing new business, the one thing that every salesperson always sells is, of course, *change*—asking prospects to change the way they're currently doing business. The irony is that salespeople themselves also fall into the 80%-20% change category. The message is that we're all fearful of change. However, it might be wise to heed the words of the legendary college basketball coach, John Wooden: "**Failure is not fatal, but failure to change might be.**"

Sales Manager to CEO:

“What if we train everyone and they all leave?”

CEO:

“What if we don’t train them and they all stay?”

Chapter 2

GO LEFT

AND

HELP PROSPECTS DISCOVER THEIR PROBLEMS AND SOLUTIONS

LET'S GET REAL

Before we start, let's first get real. Over the past few years, several studies were conducted in which several statistics were highlighted. It is absolutely critical to one's success that he/she prepares for prospect visits with these two *critical statistics* foremost in mind:

1. **80% of prospects stay with their current provider even when they are slightly unhappy** *because the devil you know is better than the one you don't know.*

2. **It cost 6 times as much money to secure a new account than it does to keep an existing one**. *Therefore, the incumbent will always lower his price when forced to.*

In other words, for every 10 new business meetings, you only have 2 chances of success! Failure to constantly remind one's self of these two facts routinely results in delivering many proposals but minimal sales.

Note:

Do not forget a third and final statistic:

3. **65% of accounts that salespeople actively work on at any given time never result in a sale!**

The entire sales process presented in the following chapters incorporates these three statistics as its foundation piece.

GOING LEFT

STORY:

When we first began working with a new client, an interesting situation arose. A company whom our client had no prior contact mailed an RFP (request for proposal) simply addressed to headquarters.

Upon receipt of the RFP, the salesperson contacted the person who signed the request and told him that he had to respectfully decline to respond to the proposal since he knew nothing about the company he could not make any specific recommendations.

The company persisted, saying that they had serious problems with their current provider and asked what it would take to get a proposal. The salesperson kept pushing back using our process, especially *Going Left* with statements like, "you've been with your current supplier for fifteen years, there's little reason to change now. If you're not totally happy, talk to their management. I'm sure they'll fix it. They'll do whatever it takes to keep a client, especially one as large as you. Furthermore, I would have to get our management approval (RFPs are very extensive). And I don't see any way I could get that approval." The company kept pushing back.

Still believing he was wasting his time, the salesperson put them to the ultimate test. "The only way that we would consider your RFP is if you would first send a team to visit our headquarters for one whole day. Furthermore, the RFP would have to be delayed six weeks in order for us to develop it." Surprise, surprise, the company agreed to both demands!

The salesperson was now convinced that he had a reasonable chance for success. In preparation for the headquarters visit, he held many meetings with the end-users. Discussions centered on pain issues and potential solutions so that headquarters personnel could address their specific needs.

The rest of the process—total involvement with the prospect—ended with a sale and a signed contract.

Footnotes:

The salesperson claimed that this was a defining moment in his career. He admitted that in his first five and a half years with the company, he was merely an order taker. He now had a system and a process that allowed him to be honest, gain instant credibility, and make good use of his product knowledge vs. simply giving feature/benefit presentations. He has continued to be among the sales leaders.

1. During one of the meetings when the salesperson was using *Going Left*, a customer service rep who was also on the call interrupted the salesperson at one point, "*Whose side are you on?"* When this was later brought to management's attention, our new client realized that a **sales culture** had to be implemented and everyone must understand (not become proficient in) the sales process—DISCOVERY—all about the PROSPECT/CLIENT.
   (This sales culture is discussed in detail in Chapter 8)

Takeaways:

1. ***The salesperson*** admitted that if he first thought that he had any reasonable chance of getting the sale, he most likely would *not have used* this process. It was brand new to him, and he had no successes to reinforce it. Since he believed he had no chance, he remained *completely unemotional* and found the process to be rather refreshing.
2. A good definition of *DISCOVERY* is "Making prospects sell *us* on why they need our products/services."
3. It helps to have "WALKAWAY POWER."

STEP 1: PROSPECT PROBLEMS (PAINS)

(Serious enough to change or just an irritant)

Determining just how serious prospects' problems are is absolutely THE most difficult part of any sales process. In other words, does the prospect have pain—something that needs immediate attention or is it something he can live with?

Example: Suppose for a minute that you stepped off a curb, stumbled and fell, and really twisted your ankle. You're able to pick yourself up; it really hurts, no doubt a bad sprain, but you hobble around. Are you going to the doctor? No! A day or two go by, it's pretty swollen; you're still hobbling, but you're still going to work. Going to the doctor? Nope!

A few more days go by; it still hurts—not much improvement. You may start "thinking about" the doctor (i.e., "If this isn't much better [by two or three more days], I should probably get it checked/x-rayed."). But as long as it doesn't get worse, you simply don't go to the doctor.

A similar situation: This time you stepped off the curb, fell, but couldn't get up, and the pain is excruciating. It takes three people just to get you up and into a car. You can't walk—it feels like your ankle is broken. Going to the doctor? You bet! Right to the emergency room of the nearest hospital.

Prospects want to be in control so they will usually offer some pain indicators—enough to get the salesperson to offer solutions or at least explain his product/service. Furthermore, salespeople get excited easily (*"This sounds like a great opportunity..."*) and too often they only hear what they want to hear. In reality, the ankle is *sprained* 80% of the time—**broken only 20%** of the time. But how can the salesperson really know? As mentioned earlier, under the dysfunctional process, he cannot.

Making the determination of pain even more difficult, consider the following example of how buyers defend themselves against *feeling* pain:

Buyers are so well protected against feeling pain that even the ways in which they describe their own pain are designed to numb it. Ask someone who has stopped at a service station to buy gasoline why he did so, and you will likely hear him answer something like, "I was running low on gas," or "The gas gauge was registering near empty," or "I needed gas." All of these statements are no doubt true, but they represent only a portion of what is true. In each case, the answer is strictly an *intellectual* one that is devoid of any emotional content. Yet the reason for stopping to buy gas is precisely an *emotional* one, namely, to prevent the problems that would develop were he to run out.

Such deeper buying motives are difficult to express because they are usually hidden deep within, often even from the buyer's own awareness. Yet if he were able to verbalize his true buying motive, he would say, "I put gas in the tank to avoid the consequences of running out on the way home—arriving home late for dinner or being stranded in sub-zero weather," and so on. Granted, people are not socialized to talk this way; nevertheless, the point is that he stopped for gas to prevent pain. Again, this is one of the two primary reasons why anyone ultimately buys anything: to prevent pain or relieve pain.

The bottom line: NO PAIN...NO CHANGE. Furthermore, failure to accurately determine pain is the #1 reason why salespeople spend 65% of their time dealing with prospects who never buy. It is not uncommon to spend 50–75% of the total sales process in this initial pain step!

The singular technique that enables the salesperson to determine pain is GOING LEFT because it allows him to *challenge* prospect's answers in a nonthreatening manner.

By definition, *Going Left* means behavior exactly opposite to what prospects expect. For example, you run into an irate customer who says, "I wouldn't buy from you if you were the last company on earth," and continues to rant and rave about his bad experience. Now, traditional responses would no doubt include, "Well, the person responsible is no longer here;" "I'm your new rep, and I promise you that nothing like that would ever happen with me;" "We've got a fix on these kinds of problems now," etc. Those types of responses rarely, if ever, change prospects' attitudes.

What if you took the opposite approach: "Gee, Mr. Prospect, I can't believe we treated you that way and I don't blame you. If I were you, I wouldn't buy from me either." At least now, you've got a chance for him to calm down and begin a conversation.

Not only is *finding* PAIN the biggest challenge salespeople face initially, but also, they rarely *spend enough time* in this step. The main reason is that prospects will generally mention at least one issue with their current situation and two problems occur immediately:

#1 The salesperson hears what he wants to hear—becomes emotional ("This sounds like a great opportunity…") and he's off to the races—feature/benefit presentations or "our solution" and ultimately a proposal.

#2 What most sales people do not realize is that they *have no way of challenging* prospects in order to determine the situation: real pain necessitating change or just an irritant that the prospect can live with. **Not being able to challenge only reinforces behavior #1 above).**

Not only does *Going Left* allow responses to be challenged, but an additional benefit is that conversation ensues, with the prospect becoming more open and more trusting because he is *not* being sold.

In visualizing this strategy, consider the circle in Figure 1 (p. 22) to be the face of a clock and apply Newton's Law of Motion. (For a sales interpretation of Newton's Law, substitute *"communication"* for motion.) Prospects expect salespeople to move the pendulum to the right, pushing toward the sale (3 o'clock) with feature/benefit presentations, trial closes, etc. **Going Left** means pushing the pendulum *back away* from the sale (9 o'clock). In other words, *stop selling* and suggest other options. One of two things will happen. Either the pendulum continues to swing to "9" and it's over—at least you got an answer—or it stays in motion moving right to "3" and the sale.

Two questions here: first, where on the clock between "4" and "8" do you think the overwhelming majority of business is lost? No, it's not "8"…it's actually "4"! In the dysfunctional sales process, the salesperson thinks that all is going smoothly. He has made a powerful presentation, submitted an excellent proposal, and now standing at "3" attempts to *pull* the prospect up from "4" with his standard closing techniques. And what happens in a significant number of cases? That's right, the communication stops—no sale!

Consider what might happen if in the above example, the salesperson moved to "5" instead of "3." "Mr. Prospect, it's occurred to me that during our initial presentation, you had asked about our customer support services and I don't think we answered it to your satisfaction…can we talk about that?" Again, the pendulum can only swing two ways—to the right, "Oh no, that's not a problem," or to the left, "Yes, we do have concerns about that" or "No, not customer service, but we do have some questions about…" Do you see how Going Left keeps the pendulum moving, which translates to **continuing the communication?**

GOING LEFT...COUNTER CLOCKWISE

BEHAVIOR EXACTLY *OPPOSITE* TO WHAT PROSPECTS EXPECT.

WHEN SALES PEOPLE PUSH PROSPECTS IN ONE DIRECTION, THEY ARE LIKELY TO *PULL IN THE OPPOSITE DIRECTION.*

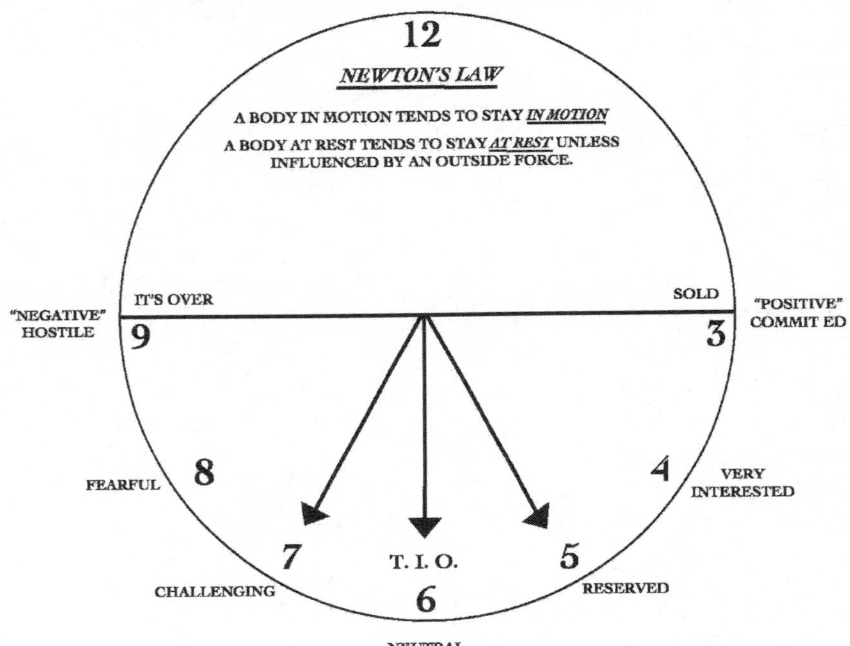

DISCUSS ALL OPTIONS OTHER THAN YOUR PRODUCTS/SERVICES

Fig. 1

Second question: how should a salesperson react to a prospect who is at "6" …you know, the one who sits with his arms folded daring the salesperson to sell him, saying very little other than "Tell me what you've got"? Once again, in the dysfunctional sales process the salesperson moves to "5" explaining all the positive benefits of his company and/or product/service. The usual responses include: "Thanks, we'll give this serious consideration"; "Send me some more information"; "Send me a proposal." etc.

The challenge here is to get the prospect off from "6" and moving (communicating). What if the salesperson moved to "7" or "8"? **"Mr. Prospect, don't get me wrong. I'm a commissioned sales person and I want this business; in fact, yours is the type of business we target and excel.** However, I get the feeling that no matter what I say or do, I wouldn't get your business." Can you think of a better way to get the prospect talking?

<u>Please note:</u> Whenever a salesperson moves extremely left ("7" or "8"), it is absolutely imperative to precede it with a softening statement (bold above). If not, the salesperson risks appearing arrogant and turning the prospect completely off.

STORY:

During one of our training classes, a participant asked, "I like the Going Left idea and believe it works, but my mind doesn't operate that way; is there any way I could learn to practice this technique?" Great question!

We asked the class to participate in an exercise:

Step 1: List the most common complaints (pains) you hear from your prospects about their current provider.

Step 2: Write the answers you believe the incumbent would give if the prospect presented those complaints to him.

Example:
COMPLAINT: Service has deteriorated.
ANSWER: "Could you be more specific or give me an example?"
(After those specifics have been given) "We'll take care of those immediately; we will also have one of our supervisors call you weekly to ensure this doesn't happen again."

Step 3: Restate your answer as if you're telling the prospect what action the incumbent would take.

Example: "Mr. Prospect, I'm sure that once your current provider found out about the problems, he immediately fixed them and even put a procedure in place to ensure that it wouldn't happen again, didn't he?

Footnote:

A good way to learn and practice Going Left is to list the most common pains along with the most common solutions; then suggest that these solutions were or soon will be offered by the incumbent.

Takeaway:

The prospect usually admits that it's an irritant (remember 80% stay with the incumbent even when slightly unhappy); or else he is in the 20% and proceeds to expand on the problem even becoming somewhat emotional.

SUMMARY

The best use of Going Left is to **discuss all other options a prospect has** (especially staying with his current vendor) other than the salesperson's product/service. (See Challenging Questions next page.)

Results:

- Quickest way to develop trust
- Keeps communication going
- Determination of REAL PAIN vs. just an irritant
- Much quicker decisions: **A salesperson's job is to get a decision "No" and "No for now" are decisions. (Sales rule #2).**

CHALLENGING QUESTIONS
(GOING LEFT)

1. Can we talk about some of the issues you're currently dealing with… anything else?
2. Which one do you want to talk about first?
3. Tell me more about that…can you be more specific?
4. The way you're doing it now/past seems to work—why change?
5. How long has this been a problem?
6. Probably doesn't happen very often?
7. Why is that a problem?
8. What's been done to fix it…and that worked?
9. What other options do you have? How much will each cost?
10. Why wouldn't that/those options work?
11. When you called the manager, he fixed it—didn't he?
12. We're not perfect either; we make our share of mistakes…why not give your current provider one more chance?
13. How much is it costing not to fix?
14. What happens if you don't do anything?
15. On a scale of 1–10, "10" being *mission critical* you have to do it, and "1" being *it's irritating but you can live with it,* where are you?
16. Don't get me wrong, I want your business; in fact, this is the kind of account we target and believe we excel, but I haven't heard enough reasons why you would want to buy from me?
17. I get the feeling that no matter what we say or do, we'd never ever get your business.

Note: The underlined in #16 is a softening statement which must precede all hard left questions (#12, #16, and #17).

Figure 2 - is a form we suggest you copy and use to take notes during the sales process. Not only does it act as a reminder to solicit more pains, but it's also a reminder to gain agreement on INVOLVEMENT *before* discussing solutions. Failure to do so runs the risk of the prospect asking for a proposal prematurely.

Figure 3 – the *PAINOMETER* is meant to show that there's no real pain until the impact questions. In the example, the RESULT is that profits are down. Most sales psychologists believe that they've determined pain when they reach the result answer. Not true—profits being down could be cyclical or temporary. Real pain lies in the IMPACT question—7A or 7B (in this case 7B)—"My job is in jeopardy!"

ISSUES—PAIN?	***PROSPECT'S SOLUTION***
Discuss all other options	**"How would you like this solved?"**

INVOLVEMENT BEFORE SOLUTIONS

Pain #1	**Solution #1**
Pain #2	**Solution #2**
Pain #3	**Solution #3**
Pain #4	**Solution #4**

Fig. 2

PAINOMETER

PEOPLE BUY EMOTIONALLY. THEY REINFORCE THEIR DECISION INTELLECTUALLY.

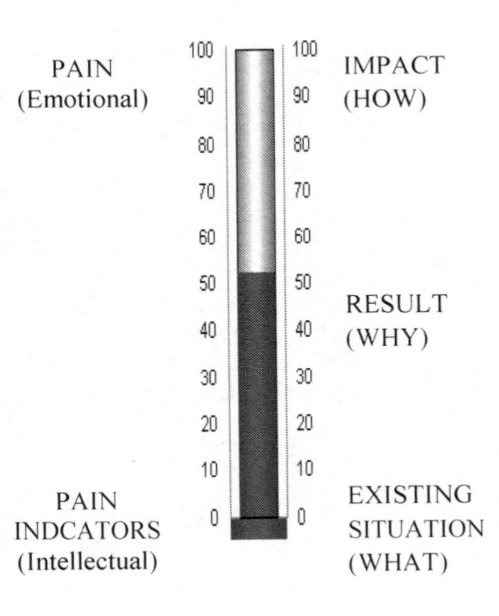

8. On a scale of 1-10, "10" being *mission critical* that you have to do it, and "1" being *it's irritating but you can live with it*, where are you?

7B. What happens if you don't do anything?
7A. How much is it costing not to fix?

6. When you called the boss, he/she fixed it?
5. Why is that a problem?

4. What's been done to fix it...and that worked?
3. How long has this been going on?
2. Can you be more specific....
1. Tell me more about that...

3 ELEMENTS OF PAIN

1. Existing Condition/Situation - What?...either something that should be done OR something that should be stopped.
   EXAMPLE: Not closing enough sales.
2. Results - Why is that a problem?
   EXAMPLE: Profits going down.
3. Impact - How will it affect the prospect?
   EXAMPLE: My job is in jeopardy.

RULES:

1. You can't move out of INTELLECTUAL unless/until prospect becomes comfortable/in control.
2. Don't stop at RESULT and try to sell.
3. No pain until "IMPACT."
4. Pain must be personal (i.e., "My job is in jeopardy.").

Fig. 3

CLIENT STORIES

STORY:

A commercial photography company got a call from a major pharmaceutical company in New Jersey. The company had just completed construction of a new building and wanted pictures.

The prospect added, "We need a real *hero* shot!"

The salesperson answered, "Gee, it's mid-December—pretty ugly out. If we can wait until spring, we can easily make it a hero shot."

The prospect said, "No, we really need it as soon as possible."

The salesperson then responded, "You know we had a similar situation a few years ago with a bank. What *they* decided to do was to wait for the first snowfall and take pictures at night with all the indoor lights on…but I'm not sure if that would be hero enough for you?"

The prospect loved this idea and a sale was consummated.

Footnotes:

1. The complexity of the job due to night—snow, no occupancy, major sign not visible—raised the final price almost fourfold!
2. The pharmaceutical company was so happy with the outcome (working together plus the final pictures) that our client company now does all their photography work.

Takeaway:

By changing just one word—*they* decided vs. *we* decided—plus allowing the prospect the opportunity to say "no" or else expand on the suggestion, the salesperson allowed the prospect to *discover for herself* this great idea.

"Humans are not ideally set-up to understand logic; they are ideally set-up to understand stories."

John Capozzi

"When dealing with people, remember you are not dealing with creatures of logic, but with creatures of emotion, creatures bristling with prejudice and motivated by pride and vanity."

Dale Carnegie

Question: In general, do people buy emotionally or intellectually? They buy EMOTIONALLY and then reinforce their decisions INTELLECTUALLY.

Example: Ask someone who has recently bought a new car why he/she bought that particular brand/model. Most will give answers such as: gets good gas mileage; rarely needs service; great safety features, etc. The real reasons: "I like this car; this is me; I really feel good driving this car;" etc.

Furthermore, it is at least three times more difficult to convince people to *reason* than to enlist their *feelings!*

An even more important consideration: whenever you make suggestions or solve someone else's problems (pains), you risk having them get other opinions because they have no emotional attachment. After you leave, they ask themselves, "That sounded pretty good, but I wonder if a competitor might have a different solution that may even cost less?"

The bottom line is that the most effective method of gaining people's attention is telling stories. Moreover, when they identify with the story, they are more apt to make the solution on their own (DISCOVERY). Now there is less chance of them contacting competitors. (Wouldn't they be shopping against themselves?)

In the last section, when a prospect told his pains, we suggested using Going Left to challenge or test his responses—PAIN or just an irritant?

Oftentimes, however, prospects honestly don't know their problems (pains) and/or solutions to those problems. The salesperson then has to help them "discover" their main issues by **PROMPTING THE PAIN or PROMPTING THE SOLUTION.**

Salespeople have no trouble telling prospects how they have helped their clients in the past, insinuating that the prospect must have these same problems. Of course, the trust factor has not been established, which only encourages the prospect to push back ("No, we don't have those issues."). Note the subtlety here…how the salesperson helped other clients…the emphasis being how good the *salesperson* is.

Let's approach this differently. "Mr. Prospect, I've had prospects come to us with…(mention 2–3 problems)."Then employ another Go Left approach " but I'm not sure if any of those are issues with you?" Do you see the difference? In the first approach, the salesperson is encouraging the prospect to agree with him vs. the second approach– he is encouraging him to *disagree*. Stated another way, the salesperson is making it easy for the prospect to disagree without getting into any kind of confrontation. In fact, very often, since the prospect feels no pressure and begins to feel trust, he or she will answer, "No, not those, but in thinking about it we do seem to have an issue with …"

Back to the first approach—if the prospect says "no," what's the next move for the sales rep? More often than not, the conversation goes down hill. However, in the second approach, the simple response is "I didn't think so" and the conversation can continue.

Suggestions:

Similar to the story at the end of Going Left, use the same list of the most common complaints (pains) you hear from prospects to help in PROMPTING THE PAIN.

Also, make a list of the primary *feature/benefits* of your product/service to help in PROMPTING THE SOLUTION.

Now, you can understand that by applying the two techniques of **Going Left and Client Stories**, you do indeed help prospects DISCOVER their own pains and solutions.

SUMMARY

Client Stories—3 Simple Steps

Step 1. "I have a client who had a similar situation, and what they did was…." (Not what we did.)

Step 2. Give your suggestions/recommendations/solutions.

Step 3. "But I'm not sure if…that's your situation…or…that would work for you?"

This last step 3 is *critical*. Not using it would be like telling a joke and leaving out the punch line! The goal is to make it easy for prospects to tell you what they're really thinking.

Note:

"Client Stories" is simply a concept. While you are using a story format, it is really just a method for you to frame your suggestions, solutions or recommendations in a way that allows prospects to "discover" for themselves.

PRODUCT KNOWLEDGE IS OVERRATED

STORY:

During a management class we were conducting, the head of a mortgage company mentioned that he had good news and bad news. The good news was he had hired a salesperson, but the bad news was he had no time to train him. He further stated that the new hire knew nothing at all about the mortgage business.

We asked a few questions. Who would he be calling on? Lawyers and real estate agencies. Could a list of lawyers and real estate agencies be provided for his territory? Absolutely. Was there support in the home office if the salesperson needed an answer? Yes. Last question, was the president a risk taker? Yes.

No time? No training! First day on the job have the salesperson memorize the following: "Hello my name is_________, I'm from _________. I'd like to ask you a question, "When you look for a mortgage broker, what specific things do you look for?" As soon as he has memorized this, give him the list and have him make calls!

Since the salesperson had little or no product knowledge, he was actually forced to listen. Equally important, his responses were directly related to the prospects' statements. The new sales rep had no other alternative, such as thinking of the next question.

The result was not only did the salesperson become a good listener, but he was also able to immediately grasp the concept of "focusing on the prospect." Remember, in the opening chapter, one of the major problems in the dysfunctional sales process is that only 10% of the focus is on the prospect/client.

Footnotes:

1. Xerox learned the truth about product knowledge a few years ago. When new salespeople are now hired, rather than begin

with a formal training program only to see significant turnover, Xerox holds off the formal training for approximately six months or until they're convinced that the new salesperson has the basic skills for success.

2. While the above experiment was highly successful, let's get real about product knowledge. The sales psychologist *does* in fact need to know product knowledge, if for no other reason than to know what questions to ask. All we're suggesting here is to put it in perspective. There is nothing wrong with admitting, "I don't know, but I'll get back to you by ________."... or "before I tell you what I believe to be the right answer, let me check and get back to you by______."

Takeaways:

1. One of the first goals of the discovery process is to get the prospects talking, and then keep them talking. In fact, the goal of conversations and presentations is what's known as the 70/30 rule. Prospects talk 70% of the time while the salesperson only talks 30% of the time.

2. There is a direct relationship between how much the salesperson knows (or thinks he knows) and how much talking he does. This is especially true for newer salespeople who believe that the best way to develop rapport or trust is to show the prospect how much he knows. Furthermore, when the prospect does talk, rather than actively listening, the sales rep can't wait to continue with his product knowledge. Usual result—30/70! (Rather than 70/30).

Note: Salespeople are frequently asked and/or offer to explain "how they are different," only to fall into the dysfunctional process—feature/benefits. Can you begin to see that **the real differentiator is our *sales process*,** rather than a reliance on product knowledge?

If indeed we're going to be sales psychologists—helping people *discover* their pain and solutions to their pain—doesn't the process begin with **focusing on the prospect?**

THE FIRST 5 MINUTES

You've heard the cliché, "You only get one chance to make a first impressions." It's true and prospects generally make their own impression within the first 5 minutes. Beginning the conversation with "small talk" on pertinent or current topics such as unique weather, traffic, news items, etc. is the norm. However, be sure to let the prospect take the lead. He/she may simply acknowledge and get right down to business or h/s may want to carry the discussion further. Just be sure it's the prospect's choice.

We have found that the easiest way to consistently get the prospect talking, then talking about h/h pain and finally becoming involved, is to begin Going Left using the two critical statistics mentioned at the beginning of this chapter: "Mr. Prospect, may I tell you a story?" I recently attended a sales seminar and the speaker mentioned two very interesting statistics. He said that 80% of prospects stay with their current provider even when they are slightly unhappy. The reason he gave was that most people believe "The devil you know is better than the one you don't." The second one was even more surprising: it costs a company 6 times as much money to secure a new account than it does to keep an existing one. What this means is that even if we were to come in with a better price, it would just make good business sense for your incumbent to match or even beat it. So maybe an appropriate discussion topic might be: "What's going on at your company that might put you in the 20%?"

STORY:

An insurance agent hired a young person directly out of college. We were concerned because he was young – he looked young – and afraid that Commercial Insurance prospects would not take him seriously. His opener: "Mr. Prospect, you have 3 choices today. The first is the easiest – stay with your current provider; secondly, if you're having some difficulties, it's still easier to work with them because they know you, and will be anxious to satisfy an existing client. The third choice is clearly the most difficult and time consuming – and that's to make a change to someone like us. Can we talk about this?

Footnote:

In addition to being quite disarming, the salesperson gets prospects engaged immediately in conversation and apparently his lack of experience has never been a factor. In fact, in his first full year, he sold *more new accounts* than the other nine salespeople in his office!

Takeaways:

1. When it's time to get to the business discussion the immediate goal is to keep the prospect talking and keeping h/h engaged in conversation.

2. As the prospect keeps talking, undoubtedly he develops *trust* and opens up enough to *discover* a real pain or just an irritant. If there is real pain, the transition to step 2: **Involvement** is much more natural for the prospect.

ACTIVE LISTENING

In traditional selling, listening is not that important since the main thrust is "Let me tell you about us" or "Here's how we can solve that." However, in the "discovery" process, listening is mandatory, since the salesperson's responses will be a result of the prospect's comments.

Stephen R. Covey's habit #5 in his book the Seven Habits of Highly Effective People is "seek first to understand, then to be understood." His basic premise is that we often prescribe before a diagnosis. Would you trust and go back to a doctor who wrote you a prescription without examining you first? As we've continually discussed, most sales people fall into this trap unwittingly, primarily due to the pressure (self or prospect imposed) to give presentations. Oh, they ask some questions, but they're usually just surface questions and treated as a simple prelude to the big show—presentation; no real listening here.

Therefore, the first step in learning to focus on the prospect/client is to improve one's listening skills—from simple listening to active listening. The better listener one becomes, the easier it will be for him to "get" information vs. giving it, thereby, reaching the 70/30 goal.

Step 1. Acknowledge Statements/Answers

Nonverbal cues or messages:
eyebrows, nodding, etc.

Verbal:
umm, uh-huh, OK, really, Oh
Good point
Interesting point/that's interesting
That makes sense
I hear that a lot
I didn't realize that
That's not unusual/not uncommon/very common

<u>Step 2.</u> Dig Deeper

Any time someone says something, two things happen: what they say and what they mean. *These two are rarely the same*.

A. Could you tell me more?
B. Could you be more specific?
C. Give me an example.
D. And?
E. I'm confused.
F. I'm not sure I understand.
G. Would you repeat that?

The responses to the above, especially E, F, and G will almost always vary at least a little from the original statement.

<u>Step 3.</u> Feedback

Paraphrase what you just heard:

A. What I just heard/what I think I just heard…
B. Sounds like…
C. If I understand correctly…

Step 4 Find the Emotion (Feeling)

People often have feelings and don't know it—they're not consciously aware. They also have feelings and know it, but do not know what the feeling is—most often denial or suppression. Rather than asking, "What do you *think* about that?" ask:

A. How does that make you *feel?*

B. How do you *feel* about that?

GETTING COMFORTABLE WITH "NO"

In order to be truly successful in sales, one of the key fundamentals that must be learned is the differentiation between *suspects,* those with no intention of buying from you now or any time soon, and *legitimate prospects*, those who will buy within the near future.

We need to expand on this last fundamental. If we asked anyone reading this book if the final outcome of a potential sale was "No," when would you want to find out? The overwhelming response would be: "Now," "ASAP," "Right away!" Sorry, but we have to challenge you here. *Intellectually,* you want to find out ASAP, but *emotionally*, most don't. Rather than encourage the prospect to say "No" and risk upsetting him, many secretly hold out hope that somehow, someway, the "tooth fairy" will suddenly appear with a signed order.

Many will argue: Why bother?...It's just a waste of time...I'm not counting on it anyway...It doesn't matter...etc. Well, it really does matter. Remember our sales rule number 2: The job of a salesperson is to get a decision—and "No" or "No for now" is a decision. It's vitally important then to bring *closure* even if it's a "No." Furthermore, **it's difficult, if not impossible, to help others make a decision if you're not comfortable making tough decisions yourself!**

OK/NOT OK

Thomas J. Harris, M.D., wrote a book in 1967 which is still on the bookshelves today entitled, *I'm OK—you're OK.* Dr. Harris makes three critical points:

1. The way people get to feel OK about themselves is to find someone else who is *less* OK than they are. For example, we can easily get frustrated, even depressed, with our job until we talk with someone who is unemployed.

2. A salesperson's job then is to make his prospects or clients feel *more* OK than he is, so that they will help him. It's surprising how many people who ordinarily wouldn't give anyone the time a day will spend extra time with someone who asks for help: "I've got a problem and I need your help."

3. However, if the salesperson makes *himself* more OK than his prospect, the prospect will get rid of him. Example: using technical terminology that the prospect doesn't understand, or acting confident that he can solve his problems—the prospect may perceive this as arrogance.

As you begin to behave "Not OK," be careful not to sound "wimpy." You still need to carry yourself in a confident manner. The transformation, however, is from "cocky confidence" to **"humble confidence."**

In summary, stop wearing the look of "confident salesperson ready to solve everyone's problems" and change into the suit of "Let's sit down and see if we can figure this out together."

Chapter 3

INVOLVEMENT

LEADING TO...

DISCOVERY

"YOU CAN'T TEACH PEOPLE ANYTHING.

YOU CAN ONLY HELP THEM DISCOVER IT WITHIN

THEMSELVES."

— GALILEO
1564-1642

STEP 2: INVOLVEMENT

STORY:

A major pharmaceutical company invited four competitors in for an introductory meeting prior to bidding. At this meeting, the salesperson from our client company read a letter he had written *twelve years* earlier, introducing himself and his company. He had also submitted a bid five years later, but the incumbent prevailed. Try as he may during those twelve years, he had no other contact.

Immediately following the meeting, the salesperson began to develop a positive relationship with the end user. However, following a bidder's conference three months later, all bidders could no longer talk to the end user. In fact, they could only communicate with the *sourcing* person. (To his credit, the sourcing person did, in fact, go to great lengths to understand the needs of his end users.)

The sourcing person also made himself available, and the salesperson kept in constant communication—many phone calls and many brief meetings even though the company was a three-hour drive away.

After the bids were submitted, the company requested a formal presentation from each bidder. The company also requested that rather than senior management, they only wanted those who would be involved on a day-to-day basis to attend and present at this meeting. The salesperson, the training manager, product manager, and the transition person were the only four from our client company to attend. We later found out that one of the competitors appeared with ten people, including top management—and they were almost immediately dismissed from consideration.

All bidders were given an agenda for the presentation. As you probably get the picture by now, our salesperson is extremely detailed, so the four spent considerable time preparing for the meeting. However, not in the usual sense of each rehearsing his own presentation, but rather how to get the audience of fourteen people *involved* in the presentation.

Following a brief introduction, the salesperson turned on the Power Point. The first slide was a picture of an elephant. “Can we talk about the elephant in the room? In your original specifications, you stated that the successful bidder must not only be familiar with the pharmaceutical industry, but also ‘Big Pharma’ as well…Well, the elephant in the room is that while we do have pharmaceutical experience, we <u>do not have</u> any ‘Big Pharma’ experience. Can we talk about that?” (His goal was not to *defend* the position, but rather have them *discover* for themselves that ‘Big Pharma’ experience was not necessary.) After a short pause that seemed like an eternity, one of the attendees finally spoke up, followed by several questions. And twenty minutes later, the company agreed. “We could learn something here; no ‘Big Pharma’ experience is necessary!”

Next came the meeting agenda. Rather than simply present the agenda in the order given them, the salesperson put up the agenda slide, and then asked for *their* priorities. Then, as each subject came up, he asked the audience their specific questions, once again getting the audience *totally involved.*

Prior to the final decision, the company requested a visit to the bidder's headquarters. Once again, much planning took place; but similar to the presentation meeting, the presenter from each department was trained in “making this about you, not us.” Once again, the visitors became totally involved. (As we later learned, the other bidders made the headquarters visit all about themselves.)

At the end of the process, the salesperson stated, “At the end of the day, I feel we did everything they asked rather than we think this is what you want.” Of course, I want the business. But if we don't get it, I have the satisfaction of knowing we did everything possible.”

Not only did he get the business, but it was one of the largest pieces of business for the company.

Footnote:

At the one-year anniversary of the contract signing, the salesperson gave out little glass elephants to all of the participants!

Takeaways:

1. The salesperson developed a positive relationship with the end user, particularly the sourcing person, by planning many short contacts—both in person and by phone—covering only *one topic at a time* rather than just a few meetings with several agendas.

2. Several of the meetings were held in a local coffee shop—short, less formal—and they really got to know each other.

3. The salesperson inquired about dress code for the presentation meeting following the bid submissions— sport coats. (The other finalists, including the incumbent, wore suits and ties.)

4. The "elephant" slide got the audience talking right from the start—*total involvement!*

5. During the entire process, the discussions centered around the prospect vs. "what we can do for you."

6. This company obviously has developed a "sales culture" which permeates throughout the entire corporation.

The major difference between a psychologist and a sales psychologist is that clients come to the psychologist while a sales psychologist must seek out prospects and develop them into clients. A secondary difference is payment. While a client pays the psychologist on a per appointment schedule, the sales psychologist only gets paid at the end following real pain *AND* a successful solution. Are you beginning to see the importance of *REAL PAIN* and the potential of spending 65% of your time and effort on prospects who will never buy?

WHEN PROSPECTS REFUSE INVOLVEMENT

STORY:

One of the companies on the salesperson's prospect list was a company he continually called on, but never even got a foot in the door. However, the company now agreed to meet with him and indeed seemed to have some unique needs. They further indicated that they did not trust that their current supplier could continue to support them.

The initial meetings were cordial, but little if any substance was forthcoming. Furthermore, the prospect seemed intent on getting a proposal because "that's what we've always done." Rather than become defensive (i.e., "we're not there yet"), the salesperson took another approach. Instead of a proposal, he initially prepared what he called a "working document"—one with several issues (pains)—and asked the prospect to rate them 1 to 5, with 5 being "must do" and 1, simply being an irritant. He then asked them to prioritize these along with several options.

This resulted in many meetings—*total involvement.* The client discovered his own needs and the solutions. The company also requested a visit to the supplier's headquarters. Once again, that visit was all about the prospect and ultimately a sale was consummated.

Footnote:

At contract signing, the new client stated, "I've never seen an approach like this—one that listens to us and then works with us to develop a customized solution."

<u>Takeaways:</u>

1. It is important to stay in touch with all prospects on a regular basis. Things change: people leave, die, get promoted; management changes; or competitors don't always perform, etc.

2. Some people don't understand "involvement" because they've never "done it that way." The salesperson got to know this prospect well enough that he could use their hot button—a proposal, which he turned into a working document in order to get them fully involved.

Not only do the best of us get fooled, but we're also faced with the situation of prospects simply refusing involvement. They (the prospect) will just say, "Just give me a proposal."

The first question to ask is: "How many proposals are won when there's been little or no communication?" Be honest! A client sales VP says he cannot think of one in his twenty-one years!

Next question: When you don't get the business, is the answer often "We went with the lower price company"? If that's the case, then here's the most important question. If you get the reputation for being higher priced, the next time the company has to get 3 bids, but wants to protect their current vendor, who do you think will get the first call to bid?

In this situation, see if this "Heart of Hearts" question will help:

"I understand, Mr. Prospect, but would you put yourself in my place for just one minute? If you believed in your heart of hearts that a process or activity was not in your own or your company's best interest, but more importantly was not in the best interest of your prospect, what would you do?"

Finally, if you're forced into a proposal, at least employ the proposal rule: NEVER PRESENT IN WRITING WHAT YOU COULD PRESENT IN PERSON.

"OK, Mr. Prospect, may I make one suggestion? Since we don't know your situation as well as we'd like, I'd be uncomfortable making recommendations in which I could appear either ignorant or arrogant. What I will do, however, is get with my group and offer several options, including pricing. While I'm confident you'll like these findings, something will no doubt be quite right. So, I'd then like to meet with your group to determine THE absolute best solutions for you. After that meeting, we'll write a formal proposal, give it to you so that you can, of course, make whatever decision is best for you. How does that sound?"

<u>Note:</u> This approach is the second test of real pain. If the prospect refuses a meeting, you must really challenge yourself—"Is there <u>any</u> pain?" Is it time to end the current activity and develop a calendar relationship?

A common misconception of giving proposals is that, "Even if we don't win the business this year, prospects will keep us in mind in the future." However, consider that once a proposal has been given, prospects' perception is that they now know all about you and your product/service. Why not give them a reason to develop a calendar relationship by not giving them a proposal so that they can really learn more about you?.

STEP 4: PROSPECT REHEARSAL

We have continually expressed the importance of *PAIN*—NO PAIN, NO CHANGE! We also discussed situations to test prospects' pain—PAIN or just an irritant? However, no step in the sales process is more critical than preparing the prospect for incumbents' counteroffers. We call it *REHEARSAL*. Once again, the Go Left technique is employed.

Assuming you did not tell the "2 statistics" story mentioned in Chapter 2 – the First 5 minutes, now is absolutely the time to introduce it. If you did already tell the story, lead with, "Remember the 2 statistics I mentioned earlier about 80% prospects stay with the incumbent and since it cost six times as much money to secure a new account, they will match any lower offer?"

The key question that follows is not, "What would you do or how do you feel about that?"—which will most often elicit vague answers. Rather, Go Left, "Mr. Prospect, **even if I were to come in with a lower price or better value, I can't see how you could *ever* refuse their counteroffer, especially when in most situations they'll even offer a credit."** (Once again, not stating this last sentence would be the same as telling a joke and leaving out the punch line!)

Of course, what you are hoping for is that the prospect becomes emotional and begins to give some reasons of why he would change vendors, and "Rehearsal" begins. Be sure to ask h/h how h/s will respond to the incumbent's *specific* apologies and/or promises. Simply think how you would respond if you and your company were being cancelled. Then ask how the prospect would answer those responses.

On the other hand, vague answers usually mean they *definitely will* consider the incumbent. So, unless there is no question that the prospect will indeed change vendors, proceed with the "loyalty story":

"Mr. Prospect, our company has been in business for __ years and we pride ourselves in customer loyalty. In fact our renewal rate the past year was __ percent. We're not perfect—we make our share of mistakes like everybody else, although we do make every effort to correct them as soon as possible. But the bottom line is I really do respect loyalty. (Softening statement) Now don't get me wrong, I'm a salesperson and I do want your business. But **wouldn't it make sense to go back and give your current provider a second chance?** Now, if he does not respond to your satisfaction, I'll be on your doorstep the next day!" (Now, you're really Going Left)!

Note: This is the one and only step that does not necessarily occur in the proper sequence. For instance, a case could be made that it could take place as early as during Step 1. As a general rule, it should be used *before* you put in a lot of time and effort. The reason? Rule #3: Be the winner or the 1st one out!

CUSTOMER CARE PROGRAM

Let's dig a little deeper. Isn't it true that most pain issues revolve around communication—a lack of it, poorly conveyed, or misunderstood? Therefore, before giving a proposal, we strongly suggest a detailed discussion (a sample is shown on the next page, but we encourage customizing). The results of this discussion should then be an integral part of any and all proposals.

An additional benefit of this program is when prospects simply ask for a proposal (not wanting to get "involved"). Emphasize the importance of communication and the need for it to be *personalized.* Do you know any company who asks prospects or clients *exactly* how they would like to be communicated with…and when? Can you think of a better way to differentiate yourself from the competition?

When introducing this customer care program, one of two things usually happen: the prospect enters into a discussion, eventually leading to some pain issues or he refuses to get involved ("Just send me the most common responses."). This of course is another test of the prospect's sincerity—serious or just price shopping?

The best way to get started with this program, especially if your product/service is renewable, is to begin with current clients. An added benefit of this visit is that it will likely uncover any possible dissatisfaction before it's too late.

CUSTOMER CARE PROGRAM

COMMUNICATIONS

A. Who—list all who need to be contacted (and by whom), then for each:

- How?—in person, phone, e-mail
- How often?
- Specific topics to be discussed?

B. Phone calls returned within.

- Normal
- Emergency (include alternate phone #)

Examples of emergencies: ______________________________________
____
____

SUMMARY:

- NO PAIN…NO CHANGE—stop and develop a calendar relationship.
- You don't have pain at RESULTS, only at IMPACT:
  How much is it costing not to fix?
  What happens if you don't do anything?
- Listening is even more important than questioning because the questions, rather than being preplanned, should flow naturally from the prospect's responses—thus, being conversational.
- Employ the strategy "Why am I here?" to get the prospects talking about their business situation.
- The "CUSTOMER CARE" discussion is a great way of getting prospects involved (without them even knowing it), which in turn can lead to discussing pain issues.
- Never forget to "REHEARSE" the prospect in every competitive situation.
- Only if pain is established should you move to the next step: INVOLVEMENT. To do so before pain offers no benefit to the prospect. Why would he want to get involved with someone he doesn't expect to buy from?
- Involvement is a true test of real pain. No INVOLVEMENT, NO PAIN. Also, in proposals with no involvement, chance of success is at or near zero.

Before we leave this chapter, you may want to diagnose yourself to see how much pain you are in– sprained ankle or broken ankle? Consider: there are many companies and salespeople who still believe the old adage that sales is a numbers game—"throw enough s--- against the wall and at least some of it will stick." Translation: give as many proposals as possible! This could work but only if indeed you have enough legitimate prospects:

A. The national average closing rate on indiscriminate proposals is 5–10%.
B. Assume an average sale of $10,000 and an annual quota of $200,000.
C. At 10% closing rate, one must send 200 proposals totaling $2 million.
D. At 5% closing rate, one must send 400 proposals totaling $4 million.

Questions: how many prospects are in your territory? How many of these will accept a proposal from you this year? Will you be able to send another 200 to 400 next year? For how many years? Or will you just dust off the prior year's proposals, sending them to the same people? Finally, how much time and resources will it take to develop 200 to 400 proposals?

How about plugging your own individual numbers?

SUMMARY of the First 4 Steps

in the

SALES PSYCHOLOGY PROCESS

Figure 4 is a visualization of the SALES PSYCHOLOGY process. In order to help clients DISCOVER their problems and solutions:

1. Realize that determining real pain is not only the most difficult step, but also takes at least 50% or more of the total process. NO PAIN…NO CHANGE—THE NUMBER ONE RULE OF SALES.

2. The most effective way to determine real pain is to challenge prospects statements by GOING LEFT…suggesting options that do not involve your product/service.

3. When prospects do not know their pains and/or solutions to those pains, rather than directly offering suggestions or solutions, use the CLIENT STORIES technique to PROMPT those pains and/or solutions.

4. The base of the TRIANGLE and the FOUNDATION of a solid sales engagement is getting the prospect totally INVOLVED in the sales process, beginning with CUSTOMIZING SOLUTIONS WITHIN BUDGETS and ending with writing the proposal together.

5. Whether a prospect actually becomes involved or not is a checkpoint on pain.

Final Note: Attempting to become a SALES PSYCHOLOGIST without mastering the two techniques of Going Left and Client Solutions is like trying to play baseball without a bat and ball.

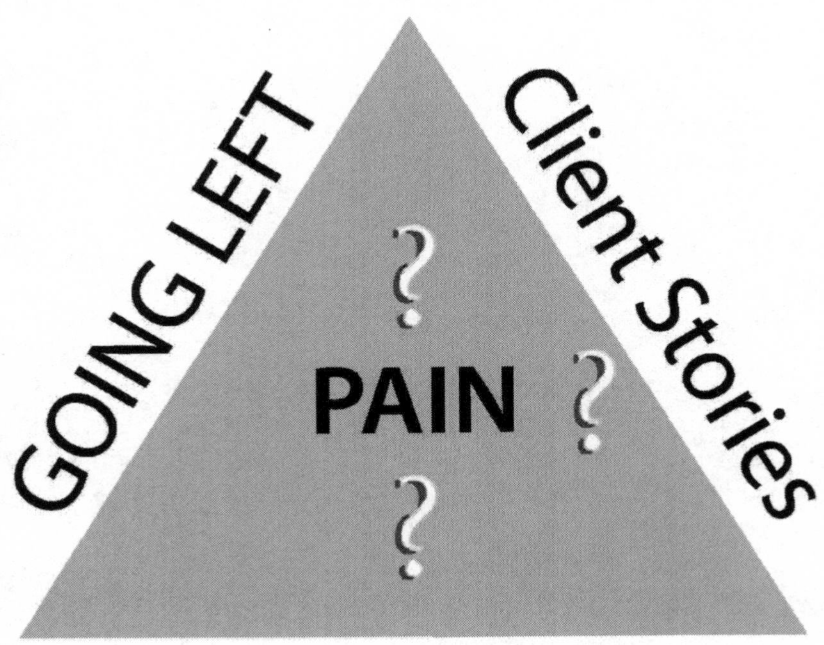

Fig. 4

Chapter 4

THE SALES PROCESS

Steps 5, 6, 7

THE SALES PROCESS

1. **PAIN—SERIOUS ENOUGH TO CHANGE?**
2. **INVOLVEMENT…GAIN AGREEMENT ON WORKING TOGETHER**
3. **CUSTOMIZED SOLUTIONS WITHIN BUDGET**
4. **PROSPECT REHEARSAL**
5. **DECISION PROCESS (REVERSE TIMELINE)**
   A. Tests urgency (Pain)
   B. Find out real issues (i.e., Boss)
   C. Business plan for both
6. **COMMITMENT BEFORE PROPOSAL…**
   "What happens next?"
7. **PROPOSAL—DEVELOPED and WRITTEN TOGETHER**
   A. Issues—Solutions—Cost Justification
   B. Prospect must know what's in it before delivery.

STEP 5: DECISION PROCESS

The previous two chapters detailed the first four steps of the sales process, namely, PAIN, INVOLVEMENT, SOLUTIONS dovetailed to BUDGETS and REHEARSAL.

This decision process is designed for two reasons:

1. The obvious:

It's a plan of action so that both parties know what needs to happen and when. For instance, if a buyer needs something by a certain date, say July 1, when does he believe he needs to order? That's right—June 30! This is especially true for the service industry, as well as products without generally accepted delivery dates. In other words, the buyer doesn't think or concern himself with "your problem"—the proper time to prepare, the right crew, equipment, etc. Moreover, few companies have an exact process, including timetables for decision-making. The salesperson is then even more in the dark and runs the risk of continually falling into the "chase" or "follow-up limbo."

2. The not so obvious:

You want to ferret out problems or potential problems that could delay or prevent a final agreement. In other words, another check on pain! How often have we found out only too late and after we've done a lot of work that the financial department refuses to spend the money, that someone on the committee didn't want to change, or that another competitor was "connected," etc.

We suggest you call this a BUSINESS PLAN and write out the developing schedule right in front of the prospect. The time needed will, of course, depend on the complexity and pricing of your product/service, but thirty minutes is not uncommon. Therefore, don't rush. You may even do it at another mutually convenient time. The decision process is actually a REVERSE TIMELINE. Here's how it works:

1. Starting at the bottom of the page: the start/install/delivery date.

2. *Working up* from this date, write in the date you need a signed order and explain why you need this preparation time.

3. On the top of the page: today's date.

4. Now, list all the steps with dates in the prospect's process. Note that he probably doesn't have a process, so all the more reason why this step is so important.

Example: "Well, I'll talk to my boss first."
"Oh, what's his first name?" (Asking for the boss's full name might put an idea in the prospect's mind that you could go over his head.)

"When can you get to him?"

"Are you sure he's not traveling/on vacation…?"
The key here is to *stretch* the time not condense it (Going Left), so that the prospect will buy and accept the dates as his own not yours. He is then more apt to keep to the dates.

"How does your boss feel about the project?"

"Is he as committed to solve this problem as you seem to be?"

"By the way, if this were your decision alone, on a scale of 1 to 10, with '10' being totally sold, where are you?" Anything short of a '10'—your contact *is not* sold. More important, if he is not a '10,' how will he be able to sell up the line? You must then go back to the pain step.

(See sample next page.)

DECISION PROCESS
(REVERSE TIMELINE)

The following example of a reverse timeline involves a national landscape company that is in the process of selling a landscape maintenance program to a prospect who recently hired a new facilities manager.

3.	Nov 3	Today's Date
4.	Nov 15 Dec 2 Dec 16 Jan 6 Jan 20	Company and facilities manager meet to design the specs (5 meetings—Friday mornings)
5.	1st wk Feb	Meet to introduce company project and service managers to review and confirm specs with facilities manager
6.	Feb 7	Sales and facilities manager develop proposal
7.	Feb 10	Deliver rough draft of proposal
8.	Feb 11	Deliver final proposal
9.	Wk Feb 14	Facilities manager presents proposal to CFO
10.	???	Day after presentation—sales/facilities manager meet to strategize if necessary
2.	Mar 1	Decision (need 2 weeks to assign crew/equipment)
1.	Mar 15	Begin spring clean up

This same line of questioning can be repeated for all others involved in the decision. Be sure that the financial person is listed in the process, and be sure to REHEARSE your contact by asking:

> "Even though you seem to favor this, why would the financial person want to make a change or spend any money?"
>
> "When he asks why you are doing this—that's a lot of money—how will you respond?" (Financial people have more control over decisions than you may think. Furthermore, many have a portion of their income in bonus, which is based on overall profitability or cost savings. Therefore, they may not be as willing to approve expenditures unless there are immediate savings.) How is your contact going to handle that possibility?

During this discussion, it is more likely than not that dates will change (reason for using pencil). Be sure *not* to change your preparation time. The prospect must decide to tighten the schedule or move the start/install/delivery date. This of course is a test of *urgency*, which is another word for pain.

If he tightens the schedule - OK. However, if he moves the start date, it could be a problem. *Decisions without urgency tend to get delayed and then forgotten.*

This process affords you the opportunity to bring up anything you may have forgotten. Example:

> "How will you tell your current supplier that you won't be renewing the contract?" This is a "must" question any time you are potentially replacing a competitor. The reason? Often, buyers get caught off guard and fall prey to incumbent's excuses. Continue with:
>
> "How would you respond when he blames his nonperformance on family or employee problems, all of which are now resolved, and. to prove his goodwill, he will give a significant dollar credit towards the next purchase/contract renewal?" If nothing else, you've at least prepared your prospect in the likely event it does

happen. The prospect has to at least stop and think—Is the story legitimate? And, is the credit enough or was a credit even offered? How about the ultimate "Go Left" discussed in the last chapter, Step 4: *Prospect Rehearsal:* "Why not give your current provider one more chance?"

When completed, tell the prospect that you'll have this typed and sent to him. It can then act as a business plan with either party notifying the other should any of the dates change. In this way, the "chase" or "follow-up limbo" is minimized. If a date is missed without notification, a simple reminder call will, in most cases, result in a response.

STEP 6: COMMITMENT

By now you must be asking, "Where's the chapter on closing techniques?" There isn't any!

This would be a good time to review Figure 1. Going Left—counter clockwise including pages 20 to 23. While it's true that most business is lost at "4," by Going Left at "5," you either identify an issue or the prospect brings *himself* up to "3."

An effective transitional question from the REVERSE TIMELINE to COMMITMENT is, "Mr. Prospect, what's the one thing that could possibly prevent us from doing business together?" If there is an answer, then ask, "How do you think we should handle that?"

When all issues are resolved, the commitment questions can now be asked, "When it's time to write the proposal, Mr. Prospect, I'll need your help. You shared with me [reading from your notes, mention all the problems/pain and solutions], is that about right? (You must get agreement.) You've also said that you'd be willing to invest/spend X amount of dollars. Is that correct? (Again gain agreement.) Now, suppose I came back with the proposal and we couldn't do all you asked and/or we couldn't do it at your price, what would you do?" (Note: This is the one time that it's okay to interrupt a prospect. The reason is that you don't want him to think it over; thus, giving *you* the benefit of the doubt here. Actually, you are preparing him for the next question in order to get a firm commitment.)

Continuing, "Mr. Prospect, you wouldn't buy from me, and I wouldn't expect you to. We spent too much time together, and, for us not to meet your needs now, frankly, would be an insult. On the other hand, assuming we could fulfill everything we just discussed, **WHAT WOULD HAPPEN NEXT?"** If there is any answer short of "we'll sign an agreement," go back to the beginning—to the PAIN step—something was missed.

Question for you: how much actual work *without* the prospect's involvement has been done so far? That's right, very little. There is no trying to figure out solutions or proposals. Just helping the prospect discuss his own problems and solutions tied together with his budget, then developing an action plan with the prospect. In other words, there is **NO INDIVIDUAL WORK BEFORE COMMITMENT!** The only closing question you ever need to ask is: **"WHAT HAPPENS NEXT?"**

Now, once again, let's get real. There will be times of course when it will be impossible to get a commitment, most notably in bid or RFP situations, especially those involving sourcing committees. Should you decide to compete in this arena, *INVOLVEMENT* is absolutely key. (Review involvement section in Chapter 3). In fact, in many cases where our clients have been successful, they were involved enough that the prospects actually asked them to help *write* the bid specs or RFP. Even though this is admittedly a lot of work, the prospect is also spending the same amount of time working with us. (More info in Chapter 5—selling to groups, sourcing committees, and negotiations.)

CLOSE THE FILE FOR NOW

As mentioned previously, we don't live in a perfect world. There will be times when the prospect simply won't commit. What should we do?

Well, we could continue to call (while making excuses for the prospect). Before you make this choice, consider the definition of insanity: "doing the same thing over and over again and expecting different results."

The other possibility, of course, is GOING LEFT. Instead of pushing toward the sale at "3," pull back from the sale to "IT'S OVER" at "9." For example, leave a voicemail message: "It appears to me that while you're interested in my product/service*, it's not high enough on your priority list* to act any time soon. Therefore, I am going to **close the file for now**, and I'll call you again in…(sometime into the future—six months/next project/next season)." *Do not leave your phone number.*

Note: "Close the file for now" is a concept. Put your own spin on it (i.e., "Let's put this on the back burner for six months.").

Before you can even attempt to execute this principle, it's critical that you not only get comfortable with "*no*" as explained in Chapter 2. But also believe in your heart of hearts *that you cannot kill the* deal. This is never a win-lose situation, but always win-win. You win if you get no response (which will happen for the majority of the time) in that you controlled the process and brought closure. You got a decision: "no" or "no for now." Remember 80% of the population can't/won't say "no." Furthermore, prospects actually *appreciate* this call since you've taken them off the hook of having to call you and tell you "no."

You also win if indeed the prospect is still interested. Most often, you'll get a return call within twenty-four hours, and one in three of those calls within an hour! A note of caution here: the call will sound like, "No, no…do not close the file, were still interested," along with a creative reason why the prospect hasn't contacted you sooner. The salesperson usually gets so excited (emotional) just to get the call that he accepts another put-off, "We'll be in touch soon," and then hangs up. While the prospect is on the phone, it may be your last chance to get a commitment for the next step—both a date and an agenda.

Sales psychologists use this principle with confidence. However, we conducted a study several years ago resulting in only 10% of salespeople using it. The other 90% still feared the "No." How about you?

STEP 7: PROPOSAL

In a perfect world, the salesperson and the prospect write the proposal together—resulting in a signed order.

However, there are two situations when this will not happen. First, an RFP (request for proposal) or a bid with *complete* specifications. In this case, refer to the complete discussion on *involvement* in Chapter 3.

The second situation is "company policy, we have to get 3 bids."

When a bid or proposal is submitted, what is the first thing the recipient does? If you answered, "Turn to the last page and look at the cost figures," you're absolutely right! Yes, even those who specifically said that price was *not* the only thing.

We strongly suggest that for every proposal or bid that you don't write with the prospect, you should develop a **TWO-SIDED PROPOSAL** (one page) and make it the first page of the proposal. Let's explain what we mean by a two-sided proposal. (See Figure 5 at the end of this chapter.)

The left side is listed with minimum specifications that will get the job done. Do not write itemized listings—keep it general—and one total at the bottom that is as low as possible.

All solutions developed together should be listed first and clearly defined. If poor communication was one of the problems, then list the solutions exactly as the prospect stated them.

<u>Example:</u>

- The project manager will meet with [NAME AND TITLE] weekly to discuss what was done the past week and plan for the next.
- All calls will be returned within twenty-four hours.
- Emergency calls will be returned within three hours, along with estimated completion time.

Most prospects don't need to see the details once they have developed trust in you. Moreover, too much detail (such as line item pricing) confuses many prospects who could get mired in the details and lose sight of the big picture. There are exceptions, however, especially a prospect who is detail oriented. The best way to handle every proposal is to simply explain to the prospect how you're going to develop it and if he needs more detail, he will tell you.

Although the total amount at the bottom must be lower than the prospect's budget or what he was hoping to spend, how much lower depends. There are three different situations:

1. If there's really no competition, just a little lower.

2. If you're trying to take the business from the incumbent – a very low number – enough to prevent the prospect from keeping the incumbent.

3. If you have no relationship with the prospect, an extremely low number such that the prospect will have to contact you.

Now on the right side, list options *not recommendations*. These are listed singularly with prices for each item and no total at the bottom. Don't be afraid to list an item on the right that the prospect expects on the left. Only do this if you are confident that the prospect will get the desired result without it. Then it becomes his choice and you've acted as his advocate—showing him a less expensive way.

Experience will tell you what to list on the right side. Just be careful not to weight it too heavily. It's unrealistic to have a low number on the left and then so many options on the right that the left looks like a car with an engine, four wheels, and nothing else.

The beauty of the two-sided proposal is that it is a total win-win for both you and the prospect:

> If low price is what the prospect really needs, he gets it while you get your profit margin.
>
> If the prospect has budget flexibility, he gets the "right to choose" without any manipulative sales techniques.
>
> More often than not, the two-sided proposal is used when there has been minimum contact. The low price is meant to be an eye-catcher, which hopefully will generate at least another meeting.

TWO-SIDED PROPOSAL

Solutions to PAINS	Options	
• ____________________	1. ______________	$ _____
• ____________________	2. ______________	$ _____
• ____________________	3. ______________	$ _____
• ____________________	4. ______________	$ _____

Minimum Specs

Total $: Must equal a number less than client's budget/shared number

Note: These are clearly options—NOT recommendations or suggestions.

* Each option is priced separately—NO TOTAL

Fig. 5

Chapter 5

CHALLENGES

GETTING FIRST APPOINTMENTS
(Cold Calls or Referrals)

STORY:

In working with one of our clients, a salesperson who had been with them for more than a year was consistently below his quota. He was, however, consistent in cold calling. He had a prospect list of well over 1000 names and he made 30+ cold calls daily. While he did get some appointments, he clearly did not get enough. He was encouraged to ask for referrals but did so sparingly.

When we talked to this salesman about his reluctance to ask for referrals, he admitted that it was much *easier* to make the cold calls. All he had to do was go into a "phone room" with his prospect list, mark off thirty calls in alphabetical order and start calling. Most often, it took only between thirty and forty-five minutes and rarely, if ever, did it take more than an hour. Referrals on the other hand took much more *planning and execution.*

Footnote:

The salesperson never did change his ways. Not only is he no longer with the company, but he is now employed in a non-sales position.

Takeaways:

1. We do recommend cold calling for new salespeople if only for a *short* time. You want to be sure of his discipline, planning ability, and execution, including time management (how long to complete the calls).

2. While referrals is the second most successful method of getting first appointments (leads coming into the company is number one), it does demand a greater amount of discipline, planning, and execution, but most important of all—**COMMITMENT!**

COLD CALLS TO MARKETING CALLS

From the salesperson's perspective, there are only three proactive ways to secure new business—networking, referrals, and cold calls. Of these three, referrals are without a doubt the most effective. Networking can be proven effective, but usually, over a longer period of time. Cold calls are the least effective. Why? Primarily due to the fact that the national average shows that 18 of every 20 calls go to voice mail or caller ID. However, there are *branding* reasons why one might want to continue making these calls.

Over the last several years, we have noticed that new salespeople are having greater difficulty in securing new business during their first year. Exceptions include those selling impulse items—with a very low price tag, and those taking over a mature territory with past success. We believe the basic reason to be the economy i.e., prospects' hesitation to buy, fear of change, and trust—"I don't know you". Therefore, branding *does* become important.

Consistency of your branding is the key here. Madison Avenue, New York City—the advertising capital of the world—taught us this concept. We call it "The Toothpaste Theory." You're watching TV and an ad for Colgate toothpaste comes on. How much attention do you pay to the ad? None! During the course of several months, you continue to see the ad and still pay no attention. Then one day, you are in the supermarket and toothpaste is on your shopping list. What pops out of your *subconscious?* That's right—Colgate! That's how branding works.

So, it is a good idea to develop a *target* market for branding from your prospect list. Those who you will call monthly for one year, leaving a short message (see "The Cold Call" script). It's been said that people won't pick up a cold call until at least the seventh time!

Because you are building for the future with these calls, it is common to "forget" them when you're busy. Fight that attitude. Since 18 of 20 calls go to voice mail, you can make them anytime between 7 AM and 7 PM!

These marketing calls of course are not the only way of branding. Monthly e-mails or postcards may even be more effective than cold calls.

<u>Note</u>: (See "The Ten Commandments of Cold Calling") For too many salespeople, cold calls have expectations—usually appointments, so failure and rejection occur frequently and can affect one's self-confidence. Marketing calls, on the other hand, have no expectations—you don't ever expect to talk to someone—they are simply branding calls.

Finally, be sure to make cold calls *simple* and customer oriented (i.e., "I'd like to discuss some industry *trends*…").

THE COLD CALL

HI, ____________________MY NAME IS ___________________
I'M FROM __________________WE'RE A ___________________
IT'S MY UNDERSTANDING THAT YOU'RE THE PERSON RESPONSIBLE FOR____________________________________?

- **WOULD YOU BE COMFORATABLE INVITING ME IN FOR A CUP OF COFFEE, ABOUT 10-15 MINUTES, TO DISCUSS SOME INDUSTRY TRENDS? AFTER THAT, YOU CAN DECIDE WHAT THE NEXT STEP IS, IF ANY. (PAUSE)**

- **DO YOU HAVE A COUPLE OF DATES AVAILABLE?**

NOTE: ANSWER TO ANY QUESTION: IT DEPENDS . . .

IF THE RESPONSE IS NEGATIVE: WE'RE HAPPY/SATISFIED, etc.

- **THAT'S NOT A PROBLEM. I'M NOT CALING TO REPLACE YOUR CURRENT VENDOR/SUPPLIER. I'M JUST CALLING TO SEE IF YOU'D BE OPEN TO SOME DIFFERENT IDEAS BASED ON WHAT YOU MAY NOT HAVE NOW.**

IF THE RESPONSE IS "NO"

- **THEN YOU MUST BE HAPPY WITH YOUR CURRENT VENDOR/SUPPLIER.** ***Proceed exactly as above*****—THAT'S NOT A PROBLEM . . .**

DEVELOP A CALENDAR RELATIONSHIP

- **WHERE DO YOU THINK THIS IS GOING FROM HERE?**
- **HOW SHOULD WE BE IN CONTACT?**
- **HOW OFTEN?**

THE TEN COMMANDMENTS OF COLD CALLING

1. **Prepare the night before.**

2. **Make the calls in the sequence you planned.**

3. **Gradually (1-2 weeks), starting with 15 minutes, work up to 45 minute sessions (no longer!) and no more than 2 sessions per day.**

4. **Plan on 15-20 calls per 45 minute session.**

5. **Expect 18 voice mails per 20 calls—the national average.**

6. **In general, always leave a message, and don't call more often than once per month. (You must have a cold call list. For example: if you make 20 calls/day, that means 400/month. So your list must be at least 400.)**

7. **No interruptions during cold calling sessions.**

8. **No expectations—no goals other than making the calls.**

9. **Some will, some won't, next! Remember the Nike commercial—JUST DO IT!**

10. **Make enough cold calls until you don't have to make them anymore. The most successful salespeople get REFERRALS!**

REFERRALS

A recent research study found that 63.4% of business comes from referrals, but 79.9% of companies had no referral system! So why don't salespeople ask for referrals? The five most common reasons:

1. I have to earn the right to ask by first making sure my client is a satisfied client.
2. Feeling that I'm begging for business.
3. The answer I always get is "I can't think of anyone."
4. I keep forgetting to ask.
5. It never seems to be the right time.

In order to get referrals, you must first **COMMIT TO A PLAN,** while overcoming the above:

1. Ask everyone. While some clients will gladly help, others may feel that they are helping you enough by buying your product/service. Non-clients, on the other hand, may feel sympathetic that they didn't buy. Also, there are many more non-clients than clients.
2. Reposition your request to benefit the referee: "Who do you know who *could benefit* from our product/service?"
3. The "I can't think of anyone" response is common. Very few people can think on the spot; therefore, you need to help them in two ways:
    - Develop a list of target accounts (usually, no more than six) show the list and simply ask if they know anyone on It. You may have several target lists according to location or vertical markets.
    - <u>Prompts:</u> "Anyone at previous companies you worked? Do you belong to a trade association, business groups, athletic/company teams, country clubs?" Be creative—the

list could be long. For each "yes" answer, ask, "Is there anyone there you can think of?" By prompting, you are helping the prospect to dial into his own memory bank. When mentioning *specific* groups, you are making it easier for him to identify a prospective candidate.

4. To prevent numbers 4 and 5 above, consider adding to your introduction: "Mr. Prospect, I'm not sure whether we'll move forward today or not, but would you be comfortable taking a minute or two at the end of our meeting to discuss anyone you know who could benefit from our product/service?"

5. You may want to consider an appointment, especially with clients. "I'd like to meet for lunch/ breakfast/coffee…for two reasons: one, to thank you for being a loyal client and two, to discuss some people you may know who could benefit from our product/service." An added benefit here is that the person may try to think of someone immediately prior to the appointment.

6. Develop a **CALENDAR RELATIONSHIP**. If you don't get a referral, don't despair. Often, it takes several times:

   "Most of our good clients have come via a referral. If you can't think of anyone right now, would you be comfortable if I added you to my referral list—those I call on a regular basis (i.e., quarterly)…Which do you prefer, phone or e-mail?"

7. One of the best ways of asking for referrals is to offer help yourself: "Let's meet for a cup of coffee and discuss how we can help each other." Don't worry about how you can help. You may not be able to offer referrals, but unless the other person is a salesperson, he probably won't be interested in referrals for himself. Examples of how some salespeople have been asked to help include a client who wanted to know a top-notch lawyer who specialized in labor law. Another request was for someone connected with little league baseball who could help his son.

PRESENTATION? BE A FACILITATOR!

Question: Are there certain audiences that truly want a formal presentation?

Answer: Not really. Even if they think they want a formal presentation, what they may really want is more structure or more detail. They may even want you to present in a certain time frame. *But you can be very informal and extremely conversational and still present in a substantive, concise, and compelling fashion.* If you ask people whether they would rather be in a conversation as opposed to a formal lecture, the answer is obvious. We are all more comfortable in conversation than any other communication format. So, why not make it an integral part of your company's culture?

Question: Is it really possible to be conversational in a presentation before a prominent group of decision makers?

Answer: Absolutely! Think about it. This kind of audience is inundated with a series of data dumps and PowerPoint presentations that are filled with numbers, charts, and graphs. They have people communicating to them in "corporate speak" and jargon until they can't take it anymore. **MOST PROMINENT CORPORATE DECISION MAKERS WANT TO BE ENGAGED**. They want presenters who are passionate and enthusiastic. **THEY WANT TO BE IN CONVERSATION**. Simply put, good speech is **GOOD CONVERSATION,** and your job as the presenter is to **LEAD AND FACILITATE** that conversation.

Bottom line: Whenever you are asked to give a "formal presentation," put yourself in the audience's shoes. What would YOU rather be involved in, a formal presentation or a conversation? The answer is pretty evident.

SELLING TO GROUPS

Most salespeople love to get in front of groups, and what else— giving presentations! The bigger the group the better the salesperson feels. His level of importance has just risen. Also, believe it or not, many salespeople get more satisfaction from giving great presentations than from closing the sale!

Unfortunately, what they may not realize is that the prospect's attitude—control, lack of trust, and all the negatives discussed in Chapter 1—is potentially multiplied by the number of attendees. Therefore, here are some suggestions:

1. Prior to the meeting, make every conceivable effort to visit, have a phone conversation, or at least exchange e-mails with every attendee. Your contact should be willing to help you by making the attendees aware of your call or at least giving you the phone numbers. If he won't cooperate here (red flag), he's no doubt counting on the group to say "no" and he still looks like a good guy who tried.

When your contact gives you the names, ask who he believes will be the "White Knights" (in favor) and the "Black Knights" (those opposed).

Your calls should say, "I understand you'll be attending our meeting on__________. I want very much to tailor my presentation to your specific issues. Would you take a few minutes and share with me your concerns, what issues you'd like us to address, or what you would like to get out of our meeting."

No problem if you can't reach everyone. You rarely will. In fact, 40% success rate is average. As long as you get one person with one concern, you can follow these steps. Just be sure to ask all those you didn't connect with to share their concerns, issues, etc., at the beginning of the meeting, and then add them to your charts.

2. Be sure to have an easel with chart paper, markers, and masking tape. If in doubt, of course, bring your own. Also if possible, ask the room to be set up U-shaped, so you can walk in the middle and get closer to the audience.

3. On the first page of your charts, list in bullet format the concerns, issues, etc., from your individual phone calls. Use their specific words as often as possible so each group member feels confident that you listened and will address his concerns.

4. Thank everyone for contributing and review each item. Ask if there's anything else to be added. If more than one page, remove page one and tape it to a wall so that all can still see it.

5. When the list is finished, ask the group to prioritize the bullets in case time runs out; at least, you'll have covered their most serious concerns.

6. Open with a simple sentence or two about your company/product/service and then proceed for the rest of the meeting in accordance with the charts.

The mission of group presentations should be **INVOLVEMENT;** that is, get the audience talking about what they want to talk about and the "presentation" becomes a **"conversation."** A good test of how well the meeting went is not how well the subject matter was covered, but rather what percent of the time did the audience talk. The goal is 70%!

POWER POINT PRESENTATIONS

Try to avoid PowerPoint presentations whenever possible. It is far less intimate than flip charts. Incidentally, PowerPoint is universally being used less and less. Why? Because PowerPoint is basically a "presentation *about us*," which, of course, is exactly opposite of what it should be—"make it *about them*."

However, there are times when PowerPoint will be necessary. For instance, a large audience and/or a large room; sourcing committees who will not allow any contact; or the prospect simply requests it.

Also, if one is really comfortable with PowerPoint and fully understands how to "make it about them"—OK—but you can still follow the above steps.

General rules for PowerPoint presentations: put as few slides as possible and no sentences (we don't want the audience to read the slides), with simple bullet points, charts, or conceptual diagrams—all of which should be designed to get the audience *involved*. Getting them involved from the beginning is critical, especially if the committee has already seen one or more competitors.

NEGOTIATIONS

STORY:

Several years ago, a salesperson was involved in a major sale with a major company. Although the deal took many months, good relations had been established, especially between the salesperson and her primary contact, the executive vice president. He was also an attorney and handled all pricing and contract negotiations.

Finally, the call came in mid-December from the contact: "Congratulations we've chosen your company. Bring over the contracts; were ready to sign." On Friday afternoon, at one o'clock, the salesperson arrived, obviously elated. Her contact met her and then asked her to come into a room, only to find the CEO and CFO, while the president was on speakerphone.

The CEO opened with, "We've decided to use your company, but we do have some issues with your pricing." (The contract involved many services and therefore was quite complex.)

The salesperson had to get headquarters approval for any changes at this point. After several calls and still no agreement, the CEO offered the salesperson a room with a phone and told her that she had "to do better." Some changes to the contract and some minor concessions were in fact made.

There was no food, no coffee, not even water—*no* breaks. Also, the salesperson had a late afternoon flight home. (Remember, it's Friday—mid-December—she, of course, had to change the flight.)

At 8 PM—yes, seven hours later—the salesperson went back to the original meeting room and stated, "You can lock me in that room without food and water, but I'm done; I'm out of here; do whatever you have to do." Whereupon, the CEO immediately stood up, slammed his hand on the table, and said to the attorney, "Sign the contract and give it to her!"

Footnote:

The salesperson, her contact (the attorney), and the CEO have a great relationship, proving that this was nothing personal, simply a tactic to get the best price. Most important of all, however, the company has the utmost respect for the salesperson and the way she handled the entire negotiating process.

Takeaways:

1. We have seen this tactic being used time and again, especially by sourcing people. The idea is to squeeze the supplier until he yells, "Uncle."

2. The more concessions one makes, the more you'll be asked to make. However, as was done here, a very small concession is appropriate, so that the prospect feels he has gained something.

3. Emotion plays a big part. Once someone has been told they have the business, they're more apt to give in.

4. Always expect to be negotiated, especially at the eleventh hour.

Strategic Sourcing committees are becoming increasingly more popular. Virtually all companies with annual sales of $2 billion+ use them; and the general average among major companies is 75%.

Negotiations by sourcing committees or purchasing departments are also more apt to occur if the product or service costs $1 million or more; or if there are annual price increases; or if a non-purchasing person chose the current vendor. This is mainly due to the perception that the *relationship* primarily influenced the past decision.

Typically, these sourcing committees look for 20% negotiated savings, meaning price appears to be the only consideration. Furthermore, if outside consultants are used, which is also happening more often, they are usually contingency paid—they only get paid in accordance with the overall savings. In other words, these committees do everything in their power to commoditize products and services. One can only imagine the dynamics between these committees and the internal company personnel.

In analyzing proposals, the committee does first of all check for *conformance*—the specs are written to level the playing field, and each bidder must complete the bid/RFP 100% or it will be thrown out. The more competitors the better it is for these sourcing committees. In order that total price alone is *not* the determining factor, sourcing committees are starting to use a "weighted average scorecard," which is also prioritized.

The big disconnect, of course, between sales and sourcing committees or purchasing is VALUE VS. PRICE. Therefore, *value must be quantifiable, provable, and guaranteed.* Why? Because of course, everyone says it. But who can actually do it? If not, then the bidder must provide case studies or references.

While training in negotiations is commonplace for sourcing personnel, there are some subjectivity (emotional) issues for these committees, which is actually determined by the negotiation process itself:

- How the seller handles the entire process (i.e., does he show empathy?)
- Management visibility
- Reasonably quick turnaround
- Flexibility vs. arrogance
- Compatibility for a long-term relationship

Note: The one question sourcing committees never want to hear is: "If we are able to give you this price, *what happens next?*" (Do we get the business?) The reason? This takes away one of their techniques, "Just one more thing…"

10 RULES OF NEGOTIATIONS

1. NEVER, EVER be the first person to give prospects the exact cost of your P/S, because you will then be on the defensive throughout the discussions. If you're forced to put the first number on the table, always give a range! The lower number should always be your approximate cost; that is, if your P/S cost $100, the range should be a little over $100 to as high as $125. How do you feel about that?

2. NEVER defend your price because you can't! (See rule no. 1).

3. Learn to develop walk away power. Always be prepared to walk away and to communicate that to the other side. When you pass the point of not walking, you lose. Plan your negotiation by drawing a line in the sand before your meeting.

4. Principle of the "Higher Authority": Always have a higher authority to check with before you make a final decision. "If I can get approval, what happens next?"

5. Anytime a concession is made, make a big deal about conceding, and then make sure you ask for something in return. If you don't, you risk getting asked for more concessions.

6. When you feel someone arm wrestling with you, make sure that each concession is smaller and smaller. A larger concession will be interpreted as you need the business; therefore, you're willing to make even more concessions. You may even take away a concession already offered, "Sorry, I made an error …"

7. Splitting the difference: Never offer to split the difference yourself, but encourage the other person to split the difference.

   Example: "$10,000 vs. $8,000—it's a shame we've gone this far…." Sooner or later, they'll offer to split the difference (i.e.,

$9,000)…. "I'll get back to you (higher authority)"…. Now, you offer to split the difference (i.e., $9,500).

8. Never jump at the first offer. Always make the other person feel he or she won the negotiation. "I'm not sure I can do it for that. But supposing I can, what happens next?"

9. Beware of the decoy/red herring—an issue created in the negotiations that will be used as a trade-off for the real issue. "We'll be hiring at least five people this year." The real issue is the money… a lower/discounted price.

10. Principle of the set aside (used when at an impasse or deadlock): "I understand how you feel, let's set that issue aside and discuss the other issues." Resolve the smaller issues and establish momentum.

THIS YEAR'S BUSINESS OR NEXT YEAR'S? (LET'S GET REAL)

As the calendar turns to year-end, it's time to get real. "Are my prospects going to order THIS YEAR or NEXT YEAR?"

As discussed, the first issue every salesperson faces is **PAIN** (i.e., are the issues serious enough to do anything about?) The only true test for PAIN is **URGENCY.** If the pain is indeed serious enough, then they will act on it now, not next year.

The best way to test for urgency is Going Left.

Example: "Mr. Prospect, we're coming into the (busy/holiday/budget/etc.) season. I'm sure you have a lot on your plate . . . doesn't it make sense to slow this process a little bit and target a decision for early next year?"

Unless the prospect **CAN SELL YOU** on why he needs to move quicker—there is no REAL *PAIN*. In spite of the prospect's good intentions, other priorities will occur, ultimately delaying the decision. Let's not wait until the end of December to find out!

The final check of urgency (PAIN) is the **REVERSE TIMELINE**. Be sure to gain agreement on the dates for all of this year's prospects!

Another time to GET REAL is when we're in the middle of a bid process, especially when things are "LOOKING GOOD."

Please remember the two statistics we've continually referenced and remain unemotional:

1. 80% of prospects stay with the incumbent even when they are slightly unhappy.
2. It costs six times as much money to secure a new account than it does to keep an existing one. (It makes financial sense for the incumbent to match any competitive bid.)

Once again use Going Left.
Example: (Softening statement) "Don't get me wrong, Mr. Prospect, I'm a commissioned salesperson and I want this business. Yours is the type of company we target and believe we excel. However, we're not perfect and we make some mistakes. But our company has been built on the **LOYALTY** of our clients. And I would hope that if things weren't right with me, they would give me a second chance. Now, you've been with ______ for ___ years, doesn't it make sense to give them one more chance? Now, should things not work out, I'll be at your doorstep the next morning!"

Another "MUST": Rehearse "giving the bad news to the incumbent."
Example: "Mr. Prospect, I know we're not there yet, but let's assume that we do win your business. Now, it's time to inform your current vendor. When he: (1) brings in key management personnel; (2) promises to take care of everything; **AND (3) even offers a credit,** isn't it going to be almost impossible **NOT** to give them at least one more chance? That being the case, why not have that conversation **NOW**?"

P.S. All the above are prime examples of **DISCOVERY**...helping clients make a decision by selling you on why they need your product/service!

Also, please remember that your job is to get a decision, and "NO" is a decision...at least for now.

TIMING IS EVERYTHING

There are very few management and sales training programs that do not emphasize TIME MANAGEMENT principles. In fact, many may know of Stephen Covey's number one bestseller: *Seven Habits of Highly Effective People*. But how many know that he wrote another book on his third habit, *First Things First*, totally dedicated to TIME MANAGEMENT?

The following is designed to make you think about better use of your own time. If you implement just these few suggestions, you will see an immediate impact, which, in turn, could ultimately catapult you to one of Covey's HIGHLY EFFECTIVE PEOPLE. However, we must first warn you: the number one prerequisite for effective use of your time is **self-discipline.**

The major issue affecting a vast majority of business people today is realizing the difference between URGENT AND IMPORTANT and URGENT BUT NOT IMPORTANT.

Examples: Urgent and important issues: crisis; deadline driven projects; pressing problems; and meetings.

Urgent but NOT IMPORTANT issues: interruptions; incoming phone calls; reports; mail; many proximate, pressing matters; many popular activities; and other people's priorities.

Too often urgency and efficiency takes the place of importance and effectiveness.

There are THREE questions here:

Question #1: What is the worst-case scenario if you do not respond to a phone call or e-mail for three hours? Before you answer "it depends," what *really* is the worst that can happen?

Question #2: Have you ever been with a prospect or client for three hours? Would you interrupt the meeting to take a phone call or answer an e-mail? Your answer no doubt is "No" [the only exception being an emergency call (i.e., "My wife is expecting…") in which case you would state the situation upfront]

Question # 3: Now what's the *real* difference in these two situations above? It's still three hours isn't it?

Suggestion: If you want to be in control of your day vs. having the day control you, check and answer your e-mail and cell phone no more than four times a day (i.e., 9 AM – noon – 2:30 PM – 5 PM. **Turn**

them both off doing the rest of the day. I know, you liked what you've read until now, but this is ridiculous! If you have the discipline, try it. You may be pleasantly surprised!

If you make the above transition, the planning section (next) should come much easier.

GOALS OR NEW YEAR'S RESOLUTIONS?

Goals provide a standard against which to measure progress. They also create the environment within which people can motivate themselves. Furthermore, if you don't implement the following, you risk the goals falling into the same box with all New Year's resolutions. Think about it: not having goals is similar to a football team playing without an end zone or goalpost.

All goals must be SMART

S SPECIFIC
M MEASURABLE
A ATTAINABLE
R REALISTIC
T TIMETABLE

1. Goals can then be a great motivating tool, provided they are accompanied by specific plans to attain the goal. Equally important, they must be reviewed on a regular basis—often monthly—and adjusted when necessary.

2. Goals should be set by the individual. However, management could prove helpful in checking—are the goals SMART?

3. Establish time frames/dates. Managers can once again help here by stretching these time frames in many situations.

Why? Because people in general want to please, and their time frames may often be short and unrealistic.

4. Another way that managers can ensure success is by establishing checkpoints *before* due/completion dates. Scheduling these checkpoints should be done at the beginning of the program.

"PLAN" DOES NOT HAVE TO BE A 4-LETTER WORD

Planning belongs to the same club as "things I like to do least."

Planning rule #1: *If you don't plan your day, someone else will!* Consider a football analogy: Can you imagine a football team with the goal of making it to the super bowl, but then not having specific plans on how to get there? Let's keep it simple.

DAILY:

1. Prepare tonight for tomorrow even if you are a morning person. Why? Because tomorrow, you are already in the emotion of the day. Possibly, you got up too late; were in a traffic jam; got a "see me ASAP" from your boss; an e-mail/voicemail from an irate customer, etc. Planning your day under any of these or similar circumstances is likely to produce a less effective day.

   The night before, however, you are totally unemotional regarding tomorrow even if you've had a bad day today. Furthermore, after some practice—no more than two to three weeks—you should be able to complete tomorrow's plan in no more than five to ten minutes.

2. List the tasks for the specific times you plan to do them. This is critical. If you don't plan the times, you risk doing the easy things first, and failing to complete your list.

3. Don't overbook; allow for "interrupt time." That is, thirty to sixty minutes late in the AM and late in the PM.

WEEKLY:

1. As with Daily #1, planning must be done prior to Monday.

2. Everything must be fully planned for Monday; the rest of the week progressively less so.

3. From your TO-DO list, fill in tasks or projects at the appropriate days *and times*, again, being careful to leave time for situations that may/will arise during the week.

MONTHLY:

1. Once again planning must be done before the first day of each month.

2. Also, from your TO-DO list, fill in tasks or projects.

3. For each of these projects, start with a completion date, and then schedule specific weeks and/or days for the task to be worked on. ***Plan ahead; schedule backward***.

Notes:

- Appointments, whenever possible, should be scheduled early in the morning and/or afternoon (i.e., 9 AM or 1 PM).

- Allow a specific amount of time for each item, *including prospect/client meetings*. Estimates will get tighter over time.

- *Quantify* all nonspecific items (i.e., not "marketing calls," but rather "10" marketing calls). These calls must be put in the sequence you intend to call—no prejudging. After each call, note any/all pertinent information and decide immediately when the next step is to occur; place it in your follow-up system.

SUMMARY:

If you have the *discipline* to follow this simple outline and stick to it, some positive things will begin to happen:

1. You will become more jealous of your own time.

2. You will think twice before jumping from one task to another, and then back to the first.

3. You will accomplish more in the same amount of time.

4. You will spend less time on non-sales duties and more time on your priorities—appointments follow-ups, etc.

5. You will gain better control over your time.

PROSPECT TRACKING SYSTEM

Before leaving this PLANNING session, we would be remiss if we didn't discuss a prospect tracking system instituted by one of our clients. It starts with a simple numbering system for each prospect:

4. Identified as a prospect but no other information.

3. At least one contact made, resulting in all pertinent info, such as all names, phone numbers, e-mail addresses, current vendor or service provider, etc.

2. Realistic chance of closing.

1. At proposal stage.

0. Decision made—sale or no sale.

The goal then is to move as many prospects as possible at least one notch—4 to 3; 3 to 2, etc.

Many of our clients use Salesforce.com, a leader in CRM solutions. Check them out.

5 FUNDAMENTAL PRINCIPLES
SALES—MANAGEMENT—LIFE

1. **FOCUS ON OTHERS NOT YOURSELF**
   - Check your ego at the door
   - Hold people accountable

2. **GET PEOPLE INVOLVED**
   - Stop solving other people's problems
   - **Help them discover their own solutions**
   - Conversation not lecture or presentation

3. **NO GUESSING**
   - Only encourages others to consider us **ignorant/arrogant**
   - No surprises

4. **LET'S GET REAL**
   - Stay unemotional; **you can't be real and emotional at the same time**
   - Say/ask what we feel
   - If we don't get real, we'll default to #3—guessing

5. **REACH A DECISION**
   - "No" is a decision (at least "No" for now)
   - A decision not to do anything IS a decision

These five fundamental principles have stood the test of time. By that we mean while they were first developed as sales fundamentals, an interesting dynamic occurred almost immediately. Our clients discovered that these same principles applied not only to management, but also to everyday life or interpersonal skills. Check it out:

1. FOCUS ON OTHERS NOT YOURSELF – *Check your ego at the door*
   Give people options then hold them accountable. And there must be consequences for bad behavior/poor performance.

2. GET PEOPLE INVOLVED – *"Let's figure it out together."*
   If a manager or parent always solves other people's problems, what is being taught? The employee/child keeps coming back for everything and never learns to be independent/creative in his own right.

3. NO GUESSING
   Guessing obviously can often lead to miscommunication or misunderstanding. Furthermore, it only encourages others to consider you *ignorant* or *arrogant*.

4. GET REAL – *Can't be real and emotional at the same time.*
   How many successful outcomes of problems/situations occur when one or both parties become emotional? Tough as it is, when one makes his feelings known, hidden agendas disappear and the real issues get out on the table.

5. GET A DECISION
   When issues are resolved, both parties are usually relieved.
   Indecision can be more stressful even when the decision is not in one's favor. At least, it's over and the person can move on. Also understand that doing nothing ("No" for now) *is* a decision.

   In summary, since all these principles are based on *psychology and human relationship principles*, not only are sales skills improved when they are applied, but management and interpersonal skills as well.

Chapter 6

PEAK PERFORMANCE

REASONS WHY SALESPEOPLE UNDERPERFORM

Until now, we've discussed the dysfunctional selling system and what to do about it. Now, let's consider the second phenomenon that prevents peak performance, one that flies under the radar of most sales managers—that is, *lack of self-confidence*.

STORY

A midsize California company had sent a letter (signed by the CEO) to one of our client companies asking for specific information. After several failed attempts to get an appointment with the CEO, the salesperson finally got through to an administrative assistant who finally arranged a meeting.

While the salesperson, of course, showed up on time, she had to wait one half hour before the administrative assistant said that it was okay for her to go in. As she entered, the CEO never looked up or said anything. The salesperson asked, "May I come in?" The CEO simply grunted, still not looking up. "May I sit down?" Same response—grunt—with head down.

Finally, the CEO said, "What have you got?" Whereupon, the salesperson stood up, handed the CEO her business card, and said, "My business card; I'm leaving. When you're ready to give me your attention, call me." The CEO sat back, smiled, and apologized. He asked her to stay and a meaningful conversation ensued, ultimately leading to the sale.

Footnote:

The salesperson and CEO have become good friends and meet socially several times a year.

<u>Takeaways</u>:

1. While the salesperson was a top performer with twenty years experience, is there a better example of the importance of self-confidence which leads to risk-taking?

2. Many instances occur when prospects will try intimidation in an attempt to have the salesperson give a feature/benefit presentation. Once this happens, the prospect feels in total control because he has all the information, while the salesperson knows little if anything about the prospect, his company, or his needs.

3. While a salesperson should never appear arrogant or act in a superior manner, it is equally important that he not be subservient. Obviously, the most successful relationships occur only when each treats the other with mutual respect.

Visualize yourself on a desert island. Just you and nobody else; no roles to play, such as father, mother, businessperson, or golfer. How would you rate yourself on a scale of 1–10 (10 being the highest)? Tough to answer? Why aren't you a "10"? The problem for many is that we are unable to separate ourselves from our roles; thus, judging ourselves based solely on our performances (results). If we are not good parents, not doing a good job at work, etc., our self-esteem will likely diminish. Lack of success alone does not make a bad person. Unfortunately, most people don't understand this concept. Joyce Brothers, PhD, tells us that we cannot out-perform our self-image (i.e., if we see ourselves as a "6," we will perform at a "6" in most of our roles). See figure 6.

The major point Dr. Brothers makes is that 80% of the population fall into their "comfort zone." Most people would like a comfortable life—good job with very little stress, earning enough money, saving for a rainy day, a nice vacation every year, etc. It doesn't make sense to "risk" getting out of that comfort zone even if they don't have all those things. "Why?" you ask?. Because should they risk and fail, that would only lower their self-image, which in turn could result in even worse results. Only the winners, those who consistently have a strong self-concept (7–10), will take risks.

Sales managers need to understand that salespeople with low self-esteem are most resistant to change of any kind, including new training, because of their fear of failure.

However, sales managers can help their people build their own self-confidence by placing more emphasis (praise) on positive behavior rather than being overly critical of poor performances.

Self-Esteem vs. Performance

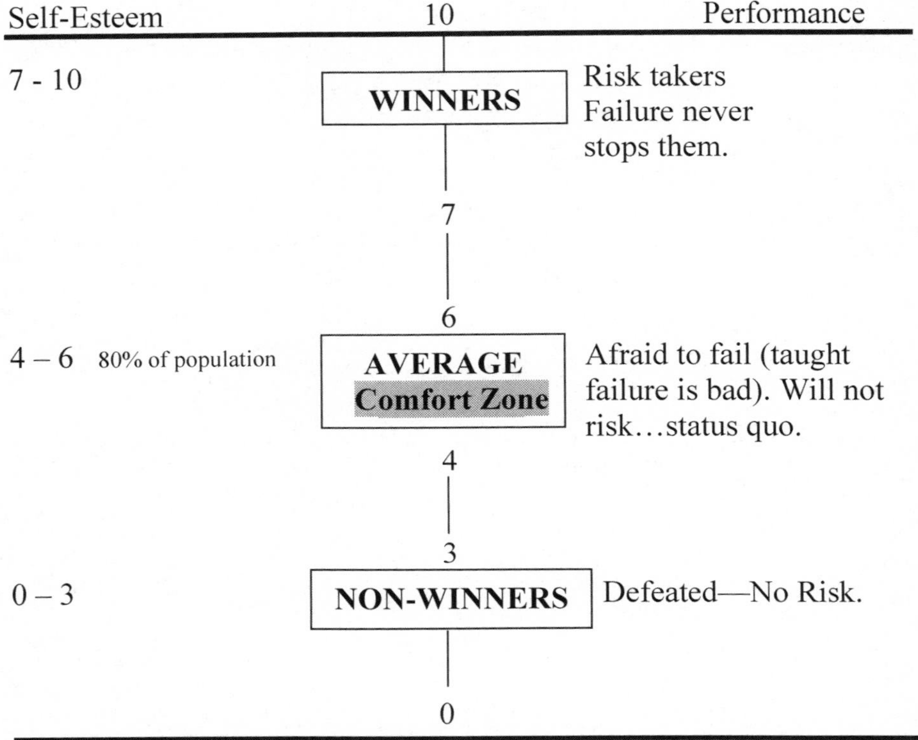

YOU CANNOT OUTPERFORM YOUR SELF-IMAGE!

- Low self-esteem creates FEAR and ANXIETY—two obstacles to success.
- If you lack self-confidence, you won't use any new training!

Fig. 6

How to Improve One's Self-Esteem

1. The biggest destroyer of self-esteem is comparing oneself to others. Set your own goals, and then measure yourself against those goals only.

2. Decide on your priorities in life (i.e., business, family, spirituality, etc.) then build your plan around that. For instance, if you decide that family is a priority, then you need to plan and make time for your family. You should realize that your business or financial success may not be quite as high as you originally intended, and you may not be able to buy the big car or the big house. However, put everything into proper perspective. As long as you have achieved your priority of time with your family, not having the car or house will have no affect on your self-esteem.

3. "When I get _______ I will be happy!" No, no, no! You need to be happy now. If nothing changes, you're still happy. Some situations could be better, but that doesn't make you unhappy.

4. Take full responsibility for everything that happens in your life.

   A. *Life is tough.*
   B. *Life isn't fair.*
   C. *It doesn't matter. You take full responsibility. In other words, take full responsibility for everything that happens in your life. Yes, things do get tough. Yes, your car was the only one on the street to get broken into, etc., but that is just the way life is; you cannot control it. Take responsibility and cope.*

5. Life has highs and lows—always! There will be bad times; however, in sales, if you get in a funk for just two weeks, it takes two months to get out of it. Therefore, double your ups and downs. Even though your downside will double, the fact

that your highs will also double will minimize your going into the funk.

6. List the successes you've had in life.

7. If there is a negative influence in your life that is adversely affecting your self-esteem, resolve that situation ASAP. (Negativity in your life drags you down faster than any other thing.)

8. Associate with winners. People you hang around with are going to have a tremendous influence on your success. (Losers hang around with losers.)

9. Accept that it is OK to fail—then learn from it!

10. Know when to be persistent. There are three types of clients:

    A. Star accounts – accounts that are high-volume, profitable, and loyal. They represent about 30% of your business.
    B. Consumer accounts – your questionable accounts (your accounts now, but there is no loyalty). While they may not entertain other vendors, if someone else comes in, they'll surely listen. So, you can't count on them. They represent about 50% of your business.
    C. Problem accounts – accounts that cause more problems than they're actually worth. They represent about 20% of your business.

    The key is to focus on the star accounts—the ones that fit your profile.

Success Breeds Success

The way to get started is the same way you eat an elephant—one bite at a time. Pick one of the above and then develop a goal setting plan around it. The goals can be either pleasure or pain. *Pleasure* means what good you will get from this; *pain* means what consequences you will suffer if you don't do it.

Attitude vs. Behavior

Most people believe that attitude drives behavior. If indeed this is true, how do we change our attitude? Other than encouragement to "develop a positive attitude," we've never seen steps or specific *plans* to change attitudes.

Changing behavior, on the other hand, demands specific steps. As you plan and then begin to implement the plan, you are subconsciously taking control, which in turn builds self-confidence. And self-confidence is the first step in maintaining a positive attitude.

If you let your attitude determine your behavior, you leave yourself open to the normal ups and downs of life with little control over the variation. Conversely, consistent behavior affords you the control to keep your attitude on even keel.

Charles Swindoll, noted theologian, author, and speaker wrote:

"The longer I live the more I realize the impact of attitude on life. Attitude to me is more important than facts. It's more important than the past, than education, than money, than circumstances, than failures, than successes, than what other people think or say or do. It is more important than appearance, giftedness or skill. It will make or break a company…a church…a home. The remarkable thing is we have a choice every day regarding the attitude we will embrace for that day. We cannot change our past…. We cannot change the fact that people act in a certain way. We cannot change the inevitable. The only thing we can do is play on the one string we have and that is our attitude….*I am convinced that life is 10% what happens to me and 90% how I react to it*. And so it is with you…we are in charge of our attitudes."

Taking Risks Leaves an Opening for Failure; Inaction Assures It!

STORY:

A small law firm disbanded upon the retirement of the senior partner. The partner also owned the building and put it up for sale.

He called our client, a commercial real estate firm, and told the salesperson that he was going to list it with one of three commercial real estate agencies located in the same town—all three of which the attorney had a business relationship. He further stated that he would simply choose the one who had the lowest commission rate (6% was the norm).

The salesperson was caught in a bind. While his instincts told him to "walkaway," the attorney was also the chairman of the board at one of his largest clients. The salesperson was, of course, fearful that the attorney might get upset; therefore, it may have a negative effect on his major client.

The salesperson stuck with his initial reaction and decided not to submit a proposal. However, he did call the attorney and explained that while he appreciated doing business with him in the past, he respectfully had to decline the opportunity to bid because he couldn't successfully complete the job at a 4% commission. (He knew that one of the other competitors had bid 4%). He further suggested that the attorney not seriously consider one of the bidders because the owner was retiring, and no one knew what was ultimately going to happen to the agency itself. He then recommended the second agency. He said that it was a solid firm and could do the job. Furthermore, he suggested that the attorney increase the commission to 6% because no other agencies would bring potential buyers for only a 2% commission (50% of the total).

Nine months later, following little activity on the property, the attorney called our client's salesperson, ultimately signing a listing agreement for the full 6% commission. In addition, a lower sales price (the price suggested by the salesperson) was also agreed to.

Footnote:

The salesperson later found out that the attorney originally was indeed upset with him for not submitting a proposal. However, he did nothing negatively to the salesperson's other major client.

Takeaways:

1. As originally stated, this was simply not a good business deal. The property was overpriced; the market was crashing; and few, if any, other agencies would work this property for a low 2% commission. However, the salesperson could have easily taken the easy way out—submitting a proposal even at a commission rate he knew he would lose.

2. However, the salesperson played it straight. He told the prospect exactly how we felt—couldn't be successful at 4%. Rather than argue a 6% commission for himself, he suggested it for his competitor. How's that for a trust builder?

3. Sometimes you have to *walkaway* in order to allow the prospect to *discover* for *himself* that he needs to get real.

RISK. *Take m*ore chances than you dare. You will make more sales than you expect. That *is* the formula.

"No risk, no reward" is the biggest understatement in the business world. It should be stated—**no risk, no nothing**. Taking chances is a common thread among every successful person. Most people will not risk because they think they fear the unknown. The real reason people won't risk is that they lack the preparation and education that breeds the self-confidence (self-belief) to take a chance. Risk is the basis of success. If you want to succeed, you better be willing to risk whatever it takes to get there.

- Failure actually occurs only when you decide to quit.
- Most people fail because they quit too soon.

Remember: “You cannot outperform your self-image.” Only 15–20%, those with a healthy self-image, will truly risk while 80% of the population seeks its comfort zone.

Do you see the relationship between self-confidence and risk-taking? Most sales managers agree that risk-taking is an absolute prerequisite for successful sales psychologists. One obvious example of risk-taking is asking tough questions.

Asking Tough Questions: If You Feel It, Ask It!

A recent research study showed that salespeople, when trained in peeling the onion, get close to the last level of questioning. And just before they get to the real impact or a measurable level, they bailout to someplace safe like, "How many employees do you have?" and "What's your current version of the software?"

Afterward, when debriefing them, the researcher asked them if they could hear in their mind what the next question should have been. They usually said, "Yes. But clearly, the other person would've felt uncomfortable had I asked that question."

When the researchers went back and asked the client, "If they had asked this question, what would have been your reaction?" They often say, "Tough question…A good question though. I would have liked to talk about that." So often, the reason given for not getting to the heart of the matter is that the *prospect* would feel uncomfortable.

The real reason seems to be that the *salesperson* would feel uncomfortable. The irony is that salespeople wait to establish rapport before asking the hard question, when in reality, asking the tough question actually helps them establish rapport!

RISK

To laugh is to risk appearing the fool.
To weep is to appear sentimental.
To reach out for another is to risk involvement.
To escape feeling is to risk exposing your true self.
To place your ideas, your dreams, before a crowd is to risk their loss.
To love is to risk not being loved in return.
To live is to risk dying, to hope is to risk despair.
To try is to risk failure.
But risks must be taken, because the greatest
hazard in life is to risk nothing.
The person who risks nothing, does nothing,
has nothing and is nothing.
They may avoid suffering and sorrow, but they cannot
learn, feel, change, grow, love, live.
Only a person who risks is truly free.

Author Unknown

You Cannot Be Real and Emotional at the Same Time

Remember, in Chapter 2, it was discussed that people buy emotionally and then reinforce their decisions intellectually.

Well, guess what? Salespeople are people, too. The problem here is that the salesperson becomes emotional more often than their prospects. Some common situations leading to emotional behavior:

- A strong referral
- Immediate connection with the prospect
- An appointment with a major prospect
- Prospect is very unhappy with the current supplier
- Prospect is very positive about your company/product
- "If I get this one, I'll make my quota; get my boss off my back; pay the bills this month," etc.

Summary: Salespeople often become emotional at the first sense of the possibility of a sale!

And the resulting behavior?

- Talking too much
- Thinking (strategizing) rather than listening
- Planning a move or two ahead
- Losing objectivity—failing to ask the tough questions

In other words, not staying in the process!

Has this ever happened to you? Here's a little quiz:

Did you ever leave a sales call saying, "Oh _____, if only," etc. (after the fact)? Why did you know what to do afterward, but didn't know what to do at the right time? You were emotionally involved…You were not relaxed and "in the moment" but rather excited (maybe even the heart beats a little faster).

Understand that emotion is the normal rush of adrenaline. It happens to everyone, even professional athletes before key games. The secret is to acknowledge it and then get back in the moment.

HIGH NEED FOR APPROVAL

Most people have at least some need for approval. Unfortunately, too many people have too high a need. Furthermore, they look to get this approval from their customers and prospects rather than another source, such as family, a hobby, boss, or peers.

This high need for approval translates to the "need to be liked." Salespeople historically believe that this need is part of relationship selling. While most of us would appreciate being liked, being *respected* is far more important. These two can be mutually exclusive (i.e., we can certainly respect someone without liking him).

This need to be liked then results in the salesperson's inability to ask the tough questions or behave in any way that might possibly upset the prospect. Three examples:

1. Even though his calls have not been returned for two to three weeks, the salesperson will not leave a voicemail message, "Since I have not heard from you, I can only assume that you found an alternate solution. Therefore, I'll close the file on this project and call you again in six months to see if we can discuss your next project."

2. The salesperson is afraid to ask any kind of "closing" question for fear that the prospect might feel pressured.

3. The salesperson is allergic to "NO." Even though intellectually he would like to get a decision so he can move on to more productive activities, in reality, he prefers a put-off or a think-it-over, secretly hoping that his "friend" will ultimately come through for him.

Note: Two Rules Here

- When you're in a think-it-over situation, the only one thinking it over is *you.*
- You lose potency every day after a closing situation.

The *ultimate irony* in all of these situations is that the salesperson didn't get the sale, *so he never got approval anyway!*

In order to overcome this need for approval, simply make a list of all the people in your life—family and business—where you could get approval. Then *shift* the approval there, so you won't need any from your prospects.

An effective manager can really help here. He compliments positive behavior to build the salesperson's self-esteem, then sets goals or standards for him to perform. In this way, approval now comes from *the boss*. One exception, however, is the manager with a *very low* need for approval himself. He won't understand the salesperson's need and rarely gives positive strokes.

THE INFLUENCE OF CHILDHOOD TAPES

STORY:

When we first started our practice, we worked with an executive search firm. Sitting in on one of their planning sessions, one of the veteran recruiters was rehearsing her call to a candidate following the completion of the hiring process. When discussing salary requirements, the sales manager inquired about the current earnings of the candidate. The recruiter admitted that she didn't know. The manager was appalled since knowing a candidate's earnings was obviously critical in any salary negotiation.

The recruiter's niche market was placing people in administrative positions within the pharmaceutical industry at salaries in the $40,000-$50,000 range. However, this position required a medical doctor with a salary of at least $125,000. While the recruiter was okay asking about candidates' salaries that were lower than her own, she was quite *uncomfortable* asking people whose credentials or achievements and income were greater than hers.

Upon further investigation, we found that she had come from a well-to-do family in the Midwest where money was never discussed. She was told not to question her family finances ("Don't worry, you'll be taken care of.").

Footnotes:

1. She never did get the placement (the sale).
2. She continued to be successful within her comfort zone.

Takeaway:

1. Anytime you venture outside your comfort zone, beware of childhood tapes.

Selling is never between you and the prospect…it's between you and your *mother!* What we mean is it has to do with authority figures. It could be a parent, teacher, uncle, coach, older sibling, etc. Right, wrong, or indifferent, we are all a product of our early upbringing, most of which we don't *consciously* recall or react to. Fill in the blanks on the following:

A. Never talk to ______________________
B. Children should be __________________
C. Respect your ______________________
D. Don't speak unless __________________
E. Money is the root ___________________
F. Don't ask stupid ____________________
G. Don't rock _________________________

Now, most probably you answered:

A. Never talk to strangers.
B. Children should be seen and not heard.
C. Respect your elders. (When was the last time you used the word elders?)
D. Don't speak unless spoken to.
E. Money is the root of all evil.
F. Don't ask stupid questions.
G. Don't rock the boat.

Why were you able to recall these (many of which are mundane) after so many years? We actually reached back into your subconscious. Scary thought? Not really. Just trying to show how much of our behavior is influenced by early tapes. Check out the following fourteen (14) statements:

REWRITING OLD TAPES

1. My business is different.
2. I need to show my prospect that I know what I'm talking about.
3. It's important that my prospects like me.
4. The most important part of the sales call is making friends.
5. It's okay if my prospects wish to think things over.
6. Prospects who think things over will eventually buy from me.
7. My product or service costs a lot of money.
8. The economy is down/prospects don't have a lot of money.
9. Money is tight.
10. My prospects will only buy if I have the lowest price.
11. Questions might cause my prospect to become upset.
12. I can't make cold calls.
13. It's okay if my prospects want to shop around.
14. It's impolite to ask people about their finances.

Here are some examples of how these old tapes will affect your approach to sales:

A. If you yourself usually think things over before making a major purchase, then there's a little guy in the back of your head saying numbers 5 and 6 are okay because that's what you would do.

B. If you usually look for the lowest price, then you'll empathize with prospects when it comes to money, like in numbers 7 to 10.

C. If you were brought up to believe that it's rude to ask a lot of questions, you'll no doubt buy into number 11.

D. If "don't talk to strangers" was drilled into you by your parents, it doesn't compute when your boss says, "Go make cold calls" (number 12).

E. If you are a comparison shopper, then you checked number 13 and will probably need help in closing.

F. If you grew up in a household where "it's not polite to ask what things cost," then you no doubt checked number 14, and, in fact, will struggle discussing budgets with prospects.

Okay, sounds interesting, but what can be done about it? Take these four steps:

Step 1. Write the outcomes you get as a result of the ones you checked.

Step 2. Write the outcomes you would like to get (see examples below).

Step 3. Get a thirty-minute voice recorder and record *your new* record collection (step 2) in your own voice over and over to the end of the tape.

Step 4. Play the recorder continually until you can't stand it—you know them by heart. Remember, the old tapes lasted a long time; it's going to take a while to get rid of them.

<u>Examples:</u> **Results I'm currently getting:**

5. *It's okay if my prospects wish to think things over.*

   I keep calling back and fall into "the Chase"…Voicemail: no return calls. "He's in a meeting," and never get the sale anyway.

11. *Questions might cause my prospect to become upset.*

   I believe that my prospect allowed me in so that he can see/hear my presentation. I'm afraid that he'll get turned off if I ask too many questions. Bond and rapport will be lost…and then the sale will be gone. Regardless, my sales cycle gets longer, and, at most times, I still don't get the sale.

<u>Examples</u>: **Results I'd like to get:**

5. When I hang in with "it sounds like it's not high enough on your priority list to make a change at this time," I will find out what *the real* problem is, or I will find out that the decision is "no" and I move on.

11. I really don't believe that asking tough questions will ever upset a *legitimate* prospect. Rather, he'll see me as a business profe*ssional, one who* is very different from all those "other salespeople." I'll *also hav*e a much better chance of knowing exactly where I stand.

Should you fail to get rid of these old tapes that are undoubtedly holding you back from your full potential, these tapes will continue to control your behavior. **Subconsciously, you'll find all the reasons why a new system or process won't work for you; in other words, you won't use the system.**

Chapter 7

FOR SALES MANAGERS

MEDIOCRE MIKE

Let's begin with a simple exercise. Make a list right now—three columns.

First column: the good employees. Mark with an* anyone you feel has promotion potential. These are the ones for delegation tasks and/or employee development plans.

Third column: the worst employees—immediate action must be taken.

Middle column: the mediocre employees. Your goal is to never have anyone in this column. They must move to either the first or the third column.

There always seems to be reasons to keep Mediocre Mike:

> "He's such a nice person."
> "He has home problems, kids, etc."
> "At least, he fills a desk."
> "I'm not paying him that much salary etc. etc."

What many fail to realize is the impact they make on the other employees. One of two things usually happens:

1. Others psychologically slough off (i.e., coming in late, not quite as responsive as when they were first hired, don't give that little extra…), and why should they? They see Mediocre Mike not being held to a high standard.

2. The good ones leave. They want to perform and want to be in the company of people who also contribute, make things happen, and help the company grow.

So who's left? You got it—more Mediocre Mikes! If you're not willing to take action on mediocre employees, you run the risk of running a mediocre department/division/company.

TIME TO TAKE ACTION ON THOSE IN THE MIDDLE COLUMN

1. Manager and Mike meet—no double talk—simply state that his performance is unacceptable.

2. Ask Mike to develop an improvement plan, usually thirty (30) days (no more than ninety (90) days). Then meet again within two days to one week.

3. The manager negotiates the improvement plan only if necessary, and Mike must agree that he can do it. "What could get in the way of you executing this plan?" Take away all possible defenses now.

4. Consequences for failure. Consequences are necessary; otherwise, Mike has no *real* reason to change.

5. Manager e-mails Mike a su*mmar*y of the discussion—action plan with consequences, so that there are no misunderstandings.

6. Every Monday morning, during this improvement program, manager and Mike meet for two reasons: first, to review last week's plan, and, more importantly, the *execution* of that plan; secondly, review the plan for the upcoming week, including any adjustments that need to be made.

Note 1 The improvement plan may or may not include actual sales. It should, however, be *behavio*r oriented, including specifics (i.e., number of calls per day with names—number of referrals—follow-up appointments, etc.).

Note 2 It is extremely important that during the entire program, meetings are held every Monday morning. Our experience has shown that one of two things invariably happens: either the turnaround happens almost immediately or the pressure of the Monday meetings wears on Mike throughout the weekends and he ultimately resigns.

HIRING NEW SALESPEOPLE

Now, let's look at the hiring process. In many companies, the sales position is the least understood position. Many executives adopt the attitude "I've hired a professional salesperson—that's one less thing I have to worry about." Recognize this scenario? You hired a salesperson. He came with great credentials. He sold a lot of business for his previous company, and you're excited! But after three months, he's sold very little. You're becoming a bit anxious and have a talk with him. He assured you that the "pipeline" is full, and it's simply a matter of time ("Don't worry boss, I've got everything under control, trust me.").

Another three months went by—no change. Now, you start thinking about taking some action, maybe even termination. But wait, "I've got 6+ months invested in him. If he just closes one piece of business, I'll at least break even. And then I'll let him go." And a funny thing happened: three to four more months and still no change. So close to a year has been wasted. But more importantly, the company is nowhere near its sales goal for the year. What happened?

First of all, you may have hired the wrong *type* of salesperson. There are clearly two types: the Account Manager who is primarily responsible for developing business from *existing* clients, and the New Business Developer whose primary responsibility is selling to *new accounts.* These demand two very different skill sets, and rarely will a salesperson possess both. Furthermore, the **New Business Developer must possess a much stronger skill set!**

5 CHARACTERISTICS

There are, of course, many characteristics of successful salespeople. However, we have found that the following *five* are the dominant ones for New Business Developers, meaning that without these *five*, the chances for exceptional performance are greatly minimized.

1. Connectivity
2. Intelligence
3. Self-Confidence—leading to risk taking
4. Passion
5. Proactive (make-it-happen) personality

1. Connectivity

Remember the old adage, "you only get one chance to make a first impression"? Well, it's definitely true for salespeople. There has to be a connection, whereby, people in general feel comfortable and totally at ease in his presence. Any hint of intimidation, insincerity, or self-indulgence rarely leads to follow-up appointments.

2. **Intelligence**

A college degree alone does not necessarily denote native intelligence. However, be mindful of the "A" student who may be *too* intelligent for his own good. Studies have shown that just as in the teaching profession, "B" and sometimes even "C" students make the best teachers and salespeople. While we recommend testing for intelligence, look for judgment and the capacity to anticipate—to see around corners—during interview sessions. A little bit of refined street smarts wouldn't hurt either.

3. Self-Confidence

As mentioned in the previous chapter, performance and results are directly related to self-confidence. Furthermore, as we've also mentioned, only self-confident people will take risks in order to achieve ultimate success. However, this trait is very difficult to measure during interviews. The best indicator is past performance (i.e., rather than how much he did sell, find out how much *new business* did he sell vs. his quota/expectations, or in relation to the rest of his peers).

4. **Passion**

   There are many jobs performed adequately, or even above average, without a passion for the job. Not so in sales. Why? High rejection rate! It's difficult to overcome this rejection or not take it personally unless one has a high belief in the product/service/company which can lead to passion. This passion then can be transformed into the final characteristic—number 5.

5. **Proactive (Make-It-Happen) Personality**

   This characteristic is perhaps *the* most important, although it probably doesn't occur without the other four. This person will do whatever it takes to be successful, refusing to buy into the usual "defensive" excuses (i.e., the economy, *prices are too high*; management, *doesn't understand our situation*; etc.). Rather, while he is grounded in the sales fundamentals, he will look for creative or innovative ways to get the sale when necessary.

ESTABLISH A HIRING PROCESS

Invariably, managers interview several candidates, then tire of the process, mainly due to spending too much time with unqualified candidates. The need to hire remains urgent, and, too often, *"the best of the worst"* is hired. Remember Mediocre Mike? Better to forget the "urgency" to hire in favor of hiring only "Mr. Right."

Note that the first three steps in this process not only take a minimal amount of time, but also rule out most all unqualified candidates!

5-Step Hiring Process

1. Five-minute phone interview
2. First interview—twenty minutes
3. Testing/evaluation
4. Third and final interviews
5. Reference checks—three—a must!

Develop expectations upfront with each candidate.
Explain the exact process and gain agreement.
If they were made an offer, would they accept and start in two weeks?

Step 1: 5-Minute Phone Call

Beware of resumes. Everyone's a superstar on paper!

The goal is to decide whom to invite for a personal interview.

A. If possible, make initial calls to candidates all at once so that you are in the same emotional mindset (five minutes per call): "I have twenty people to speak to—I'm only interviewing three. This is a call to see if you are one of the three."

B. Ask questions about their experience and product knowledge. Also, don't forget to inquire about their current earnings: "Please share with me in round numbers your current earnings." It would be helpful to use a score sheet. (See Figure 7.)

C. Don't give detailed information on any aspect of your job/company/industry at this time. A simple statement such as, "We are one of the leaders in the industry," should be sufficient. **Get them talking**.

D. Listen for their interest and any attempts to keep you on the phone vs. just giving up with an "OK, thank you."

E. Invite the top three people (based on the score sheet) in for face-to-face interviews. Schedule these back-to-back, 30 minutes apart. "We will be making an interview decision by_____. If you are still interested, please call me on (the next day)." The idea here is to set the stage for the candidate's behavior upfront.

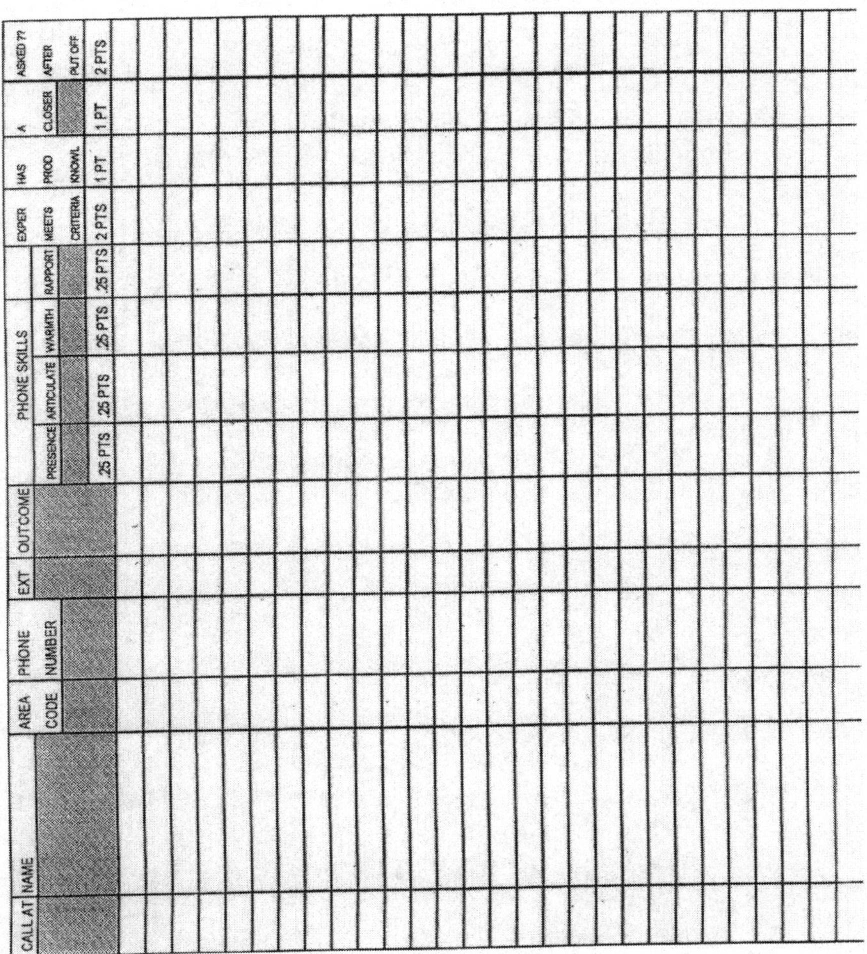

CALL AT	NAME	AREA CODE	PHONE NUMBER	EXT	OUTCOME	PHONE SKILLS				EXPER MEETS CRITERIA	HAS PROD KNOWL	A CLOSER	ASKED ?? AFTER PUT OFF
						PRESENCE	ARTICULATE	WARMTH	RAPPORT				
						.25 PTS	.25 PTS	.25 PTS	.25 PTS	2 PTS	1 PT	1 PT	2 PTS

Fig 7.

Step 2: 20-Minute Interview

First face-to-face interview should only be twenty minutes—no longer. Stay unemotional (i.e., no smile: "I've just received a rush project and we've got to do an hour's work in 20 minutes."). Check body language and just how uncomfortable the candidate might become.

Basic Questions for 20-Minute Interviews

The goal once again is to determine who should go to the next step.

That's when you *begin* to get serious about the candidate.

1. Why are you thinking about leaving your current position?
2. What are the challenges you are facing in your current position, and how are you dealing with them?
3. Tell me about the best manager you ever worked for.
4. How about the worst?
5. What are your strengths?
6. Nobody's perfect…but what areas would you like to improve?

FIRST ANSWER…REHEARSED…SOCIALLY ACCEPTABLE
ASK PENETRATING QUESTIONS…
THE TRUTH IS UNDER THE SURFACE

- I don't understand. Can you be more specific?
- Can you give me an example?
- That's interesting, tell me more
- I'm confused
- Really?
- And?

With each candidate you want to move forward with, end the interview with the following, "I'm narrowing the field for the next step—testing/evaluation. If you are still interested, call me on_______ morning. If you are one of the finalists, we'll set the testing date within three days."

Similarly, have the candidates call you at a prescribed time for all future interviews.

Step 3: Testing/Evaluation

Two important evaluations: INTELLIGENCE—any basic intelligence test; and the "DISC" model which measures sales behavior *and* the motivation behind the behavior.

Step 4: 3rd and Final Interviews

- Conduct the interview in as much time as needed.
- It's OK to sell the candidate on you/your company now, but only after he has sold himself to you.
- Get all questions, issues, etc., on the table and settle.
- Close the candidate on salary and start date if an offer were to be made..

The candidate should visit with other salespeople. Have him spend at least a half day, including lunch with a salesperson—preferably one with two to three years sales experience with your company. This not only gives you another opinion, but, more importantly, it allows the candidate to ask questions, especially about you, which he may not otherwise be able to ask. And hopefully, he becomes even more sold on the position.

DISCUSSION TOPICS

1. Family: Where they grew up, parents' occupations, number of kids in the family, where they attended high school.

2. Interests: What they like, where they like to vacation, what their kids are like. In other words, learn about their entire background/history. What are you looking for? Values? Work Ethic? Good Communication Skills? Are they Grounded? Do they get along with people? Will they mesh with the company culture?

3. Sensitivity to people: Are they oriented toward the customer vs. someone who views the customer as one who gets in the way?

4. Do they have the ability to listen?

5. Are they bright and energetic?

6. Passion: What are they passionate about? What do they dislike most in companies and people, and what did they learn from those experiences?

7. Risk Taking: How/why did they make their career decisions?

BEHAVIOR QUESTIONS

Describe a situation in which you were able to use persuasion to successfully convince someone to see things your way.

Describe an instance when you had to think on your feet to extricate yourself from a difficult situation.

Give a specific example of a time when you used good judgment and logic to solve a problem.

By providing examples, convince me that you can adapt to a wide variety of people, situations, and environments.

Describe a time on any job that you held in which you were faced with problems or stresses that tested your coping skills.

Give me an example of a time in which you had to be relatively quick in coming to a decision.

Tell me about a time in which you had to use your written communication skills in order to get an important point across.

Give me a specific occasion in which you conformed to a policy with which you did not agree.

Give me an example of an important goal that you had set in the past and tell me about your success in reaching it.

Tell me about a time when you had to go above and beyond the call of duty in order to get a job done.

With all the pressures and demands of this particular job, how exactly will you balance your work and personal life?

Step 5: Reference Checks—3

Reference checks should be done by the person to whom the candidate will report—*not* the HR department. Also, ask the candidate what each will say about him—and then compare. (See Figure 8.)

Finally:

Have the candidate you intend to hire call you at a prescribed time.

Make an offer only if he will accept your opportunity on the spot. (No "think-it-overs." What has he been doing the past three weeks?)

Consider making the official offer over dinner with his spouse or at least at lunch. How does the candidate interact with the server?

One final thought: Consider an ongoing hiring crusade. Here's why. When you're looking to hire, have you noticed how difficult it is to find Mr. Right? Doesn't it seem as though the best candidates emerge only when you're *not* looking for them? What if you interviewed a candidate with an “S” (for Superman) on his chest? Wouldn’t you make room for him even if you were forced to terminate the worst performer in the group?

REFERENCE CHECK

Candidate Name:______________________________________ Date:___________________________

Company Name:_______________________________________ Phone #:_________________________

Persõn Contacted:____ Title:______________________

Hello,__________, this is ________ and I'm (title)________________at (company)_____________________

A former employee of yours,________________________, is in the process of interviewing with our company and I'd simply like to take a quick minute and verify some of the information he/she has given me.

1. His/Her dates of employment were from __________ to ___________, Is that correct ?______________
2. When he/she left his/her earnings were approximately: $____________, Is that correct ? ____________
3. His/Her title was ______________ and His/Her basic duties were __________________________
   ____
   Does that sound about right? ____

---

4. How would you compare his/her results with others in similar functions?
   Excellent _____ Above Average_____ Average _____ Poor ________

5. Would you consider him/her to be an:
   Industrious Hard Worker____ "Enough To Get By" Worker _____Below Average Worker___________

6. Would you say his/her interpersonal relations with others on the job were :
   Very Good ____________ Average ______________ Fair __________ Poor __________

7. Were there any personal problems that prevented him/her from performing his/her job?
   Attendance _____ Drinking _____Gambling __________ Drugs______ Financial______ Domestic ______

8. He/She said the reason for leaving was ____
   Does that sound about right? ____

9. If you had an opening, would you re-employ him/her ? Yes __________ No __________

10. What do you consider his/her strong points ____
    ____

11. Nobody's perfect. What area(s) might need improvement ?___________________________
    ____

FOR MANAGEMENT EXPERIENCE ONLY

12. How many people did he/she supervise?_____________________________________

13. How does he/she operate under pressure?____________________________________

14. How could you rate his/her overall Management ability?__________________________
    Excellent __________ Above Average ___________Average_______________ Poor_____________

---

15. He/she is being considered for (describe position). Do you feel he/she is capable of handling this job ?
    ____

16. Is there anything else you would like to tell me that may help in forming an accurate assessment of his/her qualifications?____
    Comments:____

Reference: Excellent______Good_______Some Reservation_______ Not Good _______
Check Made By:______________________________

Fig.8

NEW HIRE TRAINING

Be sure to have a definitive training program in place by the new hire's start date, preferably with a written copy for him. Also, be sure that any and all abnormal behavior (even one minute late for work) is brought to his attention immediately. In other words, hold him totally accountable right from the start and only lighten up once he has proven himself.

A debrief checklist (next page) is provided as an aid in reviewing sales calls with your salespeople.

The last page contains some LEADERSHIP RULES for your consideration.

DEBRIEF CHECKLIST

Company Name Salesperson

We have had (#)_____phone talks and (#)_____Face-to-Face meetings. Today's Date______________________

I. Why is this company a prospect?

<u>**PROBLEMS**</u> <u>**DISCOVERY ZONE**</u> <u>**PROSPECT'S SOLUTIONS**</u>

1. ______________________ 1. ______________________

2. ______________________ 2. ______________________

3. ______________________ 3. ______________________

A. What's been done to fix the problem? ______________________

B. Why is it a problem?

C. What happens if nothing is done? ______________________

II. <u>MONEY</u> - How much are they willing to spend?

Prospect's budget? $______________ Range $________ to $________. I stretched it to $________

I intend to make the left side of my proposal $______________.

III. <u>**DECISION PROCESS (Reverse Timeline)**</u>

Roll-out date?__________________ Signed agreement date?______________

Steps between now and agreement date (with dates for completion)

1. ______________________ 4. ______________________

2. ______________________ 5. ______________________

3. ______________________ 6. ______________________

IV. <u>WHO</u> (place a "P" next to those contacted by phone, "F" for face-to-face)

* Contact/Title ______________________
* Decision maker(s) Title ______________________
* Committee members/Titles ______________________
* Black Knights/Titles/why ______________________

V. A. The mutually agreed upon next step is ______________________

______________________ Date ____________

B. I anticipate that this problem might arise:

______________________ and how I intend to handle it is:______________________

______________________ or I will "close the file" on ______________________

6 RULES OF LEADERSHIP

The essence of leading for execution lies in guiding an organization or a group of people, so that they not only get things done but get the right things done. There are six rungs on this ladder, but, in the end, the most important thing you can do is give your people the chance to use their strengths to accomplish their goals. This will make them feel successful. And making people feel that they have the chance to be successful is the key to motivating them to get the right things done.

1. **Establish clear expectations**. Setting specific and realistic expectations will inspire people to raise their level of performance.

2. **Instill optimism.** Confident leadership is proven to help people overcome obstacles and work more effectively.

3. **Put people in a position to use their strengths**. Discover what your people are good at, and put them in roles where they can draw on these strengths.

4. **Let them do things their way.** When you let people achieve objectives in their own way, they'll reward your faith in them with innovative solutions and energetic execution.

5. **Provide feedback**. Constantly update people on their progress, and offer them constructive criticism if necessary. People won't know how they're really doing unless you tell them. This also means praising them if they're doing a great job!

6. **Foster continuous improvement**. This is the key to a successful organization. When you expose your people to new experiences and help them learn new skills, you make it possible for fresh ideas and insights to develop, which will help your company thrive.

Chapter 8

FOR CORPORATE EXECUTIVES

DEVELOPING A CORPORATE STRATEGY

"Chance favors only a prepared mind."
— Louis Pasteur

Business growth normally occurs in four ways: acquisition; new products; more business from existing clients; and, of course, business from new clients. Acquisition and new products are not our expertise, so let's concentrate on growing business via new business.

Throughout history the traditional method of securing new business has been to hire more salespeople, have them make more phone calls, knock on more doors, get in front of more prospects to tell "our story," and then deliver more proposals. However, in recent years, this practice has met with diminishing results. Major reasons:

1. Difficulty in hiring successful salespeople.
2. Difficulty in securing first time appointments (18 of 20 cold calls end up in voicemail).
3. "3 bid" situations.
4. Prospects "shop" proposals (80% stay with the incumbent even when they are slightly unhappy).

We discussed numbers 2, 3, and 4 in previous chapters, so let's examine #1—the scarcity of good salespeople. First, consider where "sales" fits in with all the professions, including the trust factor. Not very high; in fact, close to the bottom—just above lawyers and politicians, right? If in doubt, how many parents do you think can't wait to tell all their friends, "My son/daughter graduated college and is now a salesperson?" The sad fact is that most young people who do take a sales position do so by default—they could not get any other job. In addition, these jobs usually come with a limited base salary, along with the promise of high commissions.

Since their expenses for the most part are small, these young people are willing to take the high risk/high reward position. (Incidentally, there are now eleven colleges in the United States that actually teach a course in sales—so, there may be some hope for the future.)

Furthermore, very few managers are even aware of the fact that all salespeople, regardless of their experience, have limited success selling in a virgin territory (one with no existing clients), especially during their first year (exceptions include the sale of impulse items—those usually priced up to a few hundred dollars). They also fail to realize that salespeople have to spend a good amount of their time during this first year building relationships that may prove fruitful in future years. The initial constant rejection, however, eats at their self-confidence, which in turn leads to frustration, less income than expected, and, ultimately, a different career.

What this leads up to is the necessity for corporate management to take action by first establishing a strategic direction for the company—one that will prove less daunting for their salespeople.

For example:

Step 1. Know yourself—list the company's strengths and weaknesses. Do not dwell on the weaknesses, at least, short-term; rather concentrate on your strengths.

Step 2. Identify your "core" clients—the ones who produce a major share of your total income (a general rule: 80% of business comes from 20% of clients).

Step 3. Conduct a detailed research project as to why each is a loyal customer. Be on the lookout for any exceptional customer service, specific types of personnel handling the account, and, in general, any subtleties.

Step 4. How can you duplicate this success? Vertical markets? Company size? Expanded geography? Others?

Step 5. How will this strategy avoid or at least minimize competition?

In order to accomplish the above, a strategic planning committee should be formed. This committee, usually consisting of four to eight people, should only include those who have a direct day-to-day influence on the course of the company, beginning with the CEO. The other members will normally include those who directly report to the CEO (i.e., the heads of finance, marketing, operations, manufacturing, etc.). A cross-section of personalities, thinking styles, and background is key. "Yes men" or those who think alike are not likely to *challenge* ideas, which is critical to the development of a realistic strategy.

Who will lead this group is also key. This person should not be the CEO. Rather he or she should be a facilitator—one who can lead the process, but not actively participate in the give-and-take of setting strategy. This person can come from inside the company, but, in many cases, an outsider may be more practical.

Some guidelines:

- Meetings with key clients may be appropriate. Their subtle insight into the relationship could prove helpful. The biggest issues most likely will occur when you mix facts with assumptions.

  Example: assuming that past trends, positive as well as negative will continue. Therefore, be sure to review all solutions on a regular basis (quarterly?).

- Get real. While it may be nice to think positively, a strategy developed without all potential negatives being seriously considered is not likely to be very successful.

- Strategy development works best when it is a process over time. Meetings every two to three weeks over six months are generally appropriate. This assumes that there is enough time between meetings for the participants to handle their individual assignments in addition to their regular duties.

- Once the corporate strategy is set in place, it should be reviewed, at least, once a year. As we all know, things do change. And when they do, the committee must not be afraid to make necessary adjustments.

A question that's always asked is, "How can we be assured that this strategy is realistic?" Ask yourself these four questions:

1. Do we have the knowledge, skills, and processes?
2. Is there real value for the client?
3. Have we differentiated ourselves from the competition?
4. Have we made it difficult to copy?

The chances are you will not be able to answer "yes" to all four. The next section will explain.

ESTABLISHING A SALES CULTURE

Throughout this book, we've mentioned traditional selling and its associated problems, especially in securing new business:

- A dysfunctional selling process
- Too few highly skilled salespeople
- Difficulty in hiring successful salespeople
- The 1/3 theory—in a typical sales force, 1/3 are successful, 1/3 are mediocre, and 1/3 should not be there.

We're now adding one more: **not maximizing the strengths of the highly skilled sales professional**. For instance, there seems to be a direct relationship between the skill of a salesperson and his ability to do paperwork (the more skilled a salesperson is the less effective he is at paperwork). Yet think about how much more paperwork is demanded from salespeople today compared with just a few years ago. In fact, recently, a client compiled a report which showed that the average salesperson spends the equivalent of 14 days/year in internal meetings and 45 days/year in administrative work—almost 2 full months annually!

So, the question becomes how can the #1 asset of the highly skilled salesperson be maximized? This skill, of course, is his "connectivity," or his interpersonal skills leading to relationship building and prospect involvement.

First of all, STOP HIRING! In fact *reduce* the number of salespeople. (Review Chapter 7—"Mediocre Mike.") Consider replacing them with sales support personnel. Sales support people can wear many hats, depending on several circumstances (i.e., complementing the salesperson's weaknesses, customer service needs, product knowledge awareness, etc.). They can take on such duties, but not limited to:

- Cold calls for first appointments
- Writing/developing proposals
- Day-to-day client responsibility
- Handling or delegating incoming phone calls and e-mails
- Accompanying salespeople on specific calls
- General administrative duties

The immediate result of this process is that the successful salesperson assumes a much larger territory or account base with an imminent increase in sales. However, there is a by-product which can enhance the future. There is little doubt that a salesperson hired from *within* the company has a much better chance of success than someone hired outside the company. Therefore, when hiring sales support people, look for their connectivity or positive interpersonal skills. A future move into sales could then be a natural career opportunity.

An added benefit to this approach is that there should *not* be any additional budget requirements. In fact, in many cases, the overall sales budget can be *reduced.*

Hiring sales support personnel is only step one in developing a company sales culture. Step two is equally important; however, it is a little more daunting. The traditional top-down reporting structure often protects and promotes individual "silos" (how often have we seen marketing and sales go their own separate ways). We are suggesting that all departments having any connection with sales not only work together, but also report either directly or indirectly to one person (i.e., Vice President of Sales). (See figure 9.)

The salesperson then manages the entire process. He decides who should attend meetings and the exact role each should play. The emphasis is on customer service or proving *value* to the client.

While sales support people do not need to attend all sales training sessions, they do need to be familiar with the sales process. Not only should they understand the salesperson's behavior, but they also need to embrace and practice making presentations *about the prospect*, not about the company's products and services. They also need to learn how to get prospects *involved* in conversation; thus, keeping in sync with the salesperson.

As you can see, once everyone has at least a working knowledge of the sales process, a united front becomes commonplace—one that will be very difficult for competition to duplicate.

When a company-wide "sales culture" has been instituted, can you now answer "yes" to the four questions in the last section?

In summary, the thrust of this book is aimed at the **selling process**, but no matter how skilled your salespeople are, the only way they can reach their ultimate potential—and, in turn, for the company to reach its growth goals—is to **develop a strategy** aimed at target markets, **and install a sales culture** that maximizes your resources.

For detailed information on developing corporate strategies and building a sales culture, we suggest the book "On Your Mark…Get Set…Grow!" by Tom Donato.

"It is not a question of how well each process works; the question is how well they work together."

—Lloyd Dobens

360^0 Sales Organization

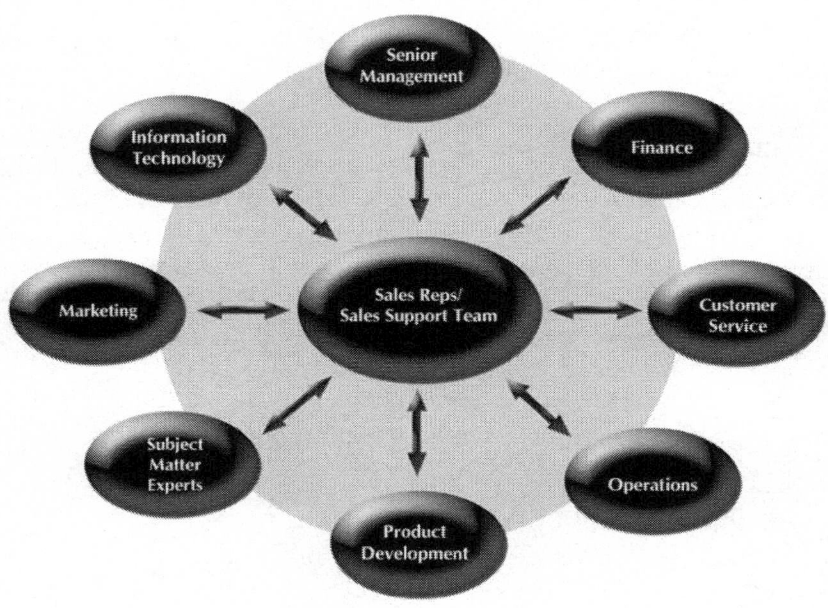

Fig. 9

Chapter 9

FOOD FOR THOUGHT

Randy Pausch was a professor at Carnegie Mellon. He was diagnosed with pancreatic cancer in September 2006. One year later, he gave the popular seventy-six-minute speech to his class called, "The Last Lecture." Worried that his wife and three children would not be cared for as he would have wanted, he wrote a book with the same title. It immediately rose to the top of the nonfiction bestseller list, and reaped more than $6 million. He died ten months after giving the speech at age forty-seven.

My library consists of over 100 sales and management books. However, I believe that this book is something special, not only because of his personal story, but also because of his powerful messages in various aspects of life. Here are some excerpts. See if you agree. (I've also included some other information for your consideration.)

THE LAST LECTURE

By Randy Pausch

If you dispense your own wisdom, others often dismiss it; if you offer wisdom from a third party, it seems less arrogant and acceptable.

Everybody loves telling stories. It's one of the truly universal things about our species.

Phrase alternatives as questions: Instead of "I think we should do A, not B," try "What if we did A, instead of B?" That allows people to offer comments rather than defend one choice.

Coach Graham worked in a no-coddling zone. Self-esteem? He knew there was really only one way to teach kids how to develop it: You give them something they can't do, they work hard until they find they can do it, and you just keep repeating the process.

Leadership is the distilled essence of a dynamic manager, a guy who knows how to delegate, has the passion to inspire, and looks good in what he wears to work. He is in charge of morale.

The brick walls are there for a reason. They're not there to keep us out. The brick walls are there to give us a chance to show how badly we want something.

It's easy to look smart when you're parroting smart people.

When people perceive you as being so arrogant, it's going to limit what you're going to be able to accomplish in life.

The only way any of us can improve is if we develop a real ability to assess ourselves. If we can't accurately do that, how can we tell if we're getting better or worse?

Getting people to welcome feedback was the hardest thing I ever had to do as an educator.

When they talk of building self-esteem, they often resort to empty flattery rather than character-building honesty.

Smart isn't enough. The kind of people I want on my team are those who help everyone else feel happy to be here.

Too many people go through life complaining about problems. I've always believed that if you took one-tenth the energy you put into complaining and applied it to solving the problem, you'd be surprised by how well things can work out.

Complaining does not work as a strategy. We all have infinite time and energy. Any time we spend whining is unlikely to help us achieve our goals. And it won't make us happier.

Experience is what you get when you didn't get what you wanted. It's a phrase worth considering at every brick wall we encounter, and at every disappointment. It's also a reminder that failure is not just acceptable it's often essential.

The best way to prepare is to think negatively. Yes, I'm a great optimist, but when trying to make a decision, I often think of the worst-case scenario. Be a poster boy for "the healthy balance between optimism and reality."

Proper apologies have three parts:

1. What I did was wrong.
2. I feel badly that I hurt you.
3. How do I make this better?

If I could only give three words of advice, they would be "tell the truth." If I got three more words, I'd add: "All the time." Parents taught us that "you're only as good as your word," and there's no better way to say it.

The best care-giving advice we've ever heard comes from flight attendants: "Put on your own oxygen mask before assisting others."

CONSIDER

1. Socrates was called, "an immoral corrupter of youth."

2. An expert said of Vince Lombardi, "He possesses minimal football knowledge; lacks motivation."

3. Beethoven handled the violin awkwardly and preferred playing his own compositions instead of improving his technique. His teacher called him hopeless as a composer.

4. The parents of the famous opera singer Enrico Caruso wanted him to be an engineer. His teacher said he had no voice at all and could not sing.

5. Walt Disney was fired by a newspaper editor for lack of ideas. He also went bankrupt several times before he built Disneyland.

6. Thomas Edison's teachers said he was too stupid to learn anything. Moreover, when he invented the light bulb, he tried over 2000 experiments before he got it to work. A young reporter asked him how it felt to fail so many times. He said, "I never failed once. I invented the light bulb. It just happened to be a 2000 step process."

7. In the 1940s, another young inventor took his idea to twenty corporations, including some of the biggest in the country. They all turned him down. After seven long years of rejections, he finally got a tiny company in Rochester, New York, the Haloid company, to purchase the rights of his invention—later known as the Xerox plain paper copier.

8. Henry Ford failed and went broke five times before he finally succeeded.

9. Malcolm Forbes Sr., father of Steve Forbes, presidential candidate, founder and the late editor-in-chief of *Forbes* magazine, one of the most successful business publications in the world, failed to make

the staff of the school newspaper when he was an undergraduate at Princeton University.

10. Albert Einstein, man of the century, did not speak until he was four years old and didn't read until he was seven. His teacher described him as “mentally slow, unsociable and adrift forever in his foolish dreams.” He was expelled from one school and refused admittance to another.

15 MISTAKES SALESPEOPLE MAKE

1. **ALWAYS SELLING**
2. **LIKE TO TALK**
3. **INFORMATION GIVERS**
4. **NEED TO BE UNDERSTOOD**
5. **GUESS WHAT OTHERS ARE THINKING**
6. **GIVE FEATURE BENEFIT PRESENTATIONS**
7. **ANSWER OBJECTIONS**
8. **TELL WHAT THE PRODUCT/SERVICE COSTS**
9. **SOLVE PROSPECTS' PROBLEMS**
10. **DEVELOP PROPOSALS TO SECURE BUSINESS**
11. **USE CLOSING TECHNIQUES**
12. **LIVE IN "FOLLOW-UP LIMBO"**
13. **IT'S OK IF PROSPECT CONTROLS THE PROCESS**
14. **NO SALE = PERSONAL REJECTION**
15. **NEED THE SALE**

10 BUSINESS HABITS

1. **THERE IS NO GROWTH WITHOUT PAIN.**
2. **IT IS EASIER TO ADJUST TO THE HARDSHIP OF A POOR LIVING, THAN IT IS TO ADJUST TO THE HARDSHIP OF MAKING A BETTER ONE!**
3. **THE BIGGEST PRODUCERS *DO* THE THINGS THEY DON'T LIKE TO DO.**
4. **IT TAKES 21 DAYS TO CHANGE OR DEVELOP A HABIT …USUALLY INCLUDES 2–3 SLIP-UPS.**
5. **FAILURE ONLY OCCURS WHEN YOU DECIDE TO QUIT—MOST FAIL BECAUSE THEY QUIT TOO SOON.**
6. **FAILURE: "THE WALLENDA FACTOR." WHEN KARL FELL, ALL HE THOUGHT ABOUT WAS NOT FALLING RATHER THAN CONCENTRATING ON WALKING THE TIGHTROPE.**
7. **REMEMBER THE 6 W'S:**
   WORKING WILL WIN WHEN WISHING WON'T.
8. **NO RISK—NO NOTHING. BEHOLD THE TURTLE; HE MAKES PROGRESS ONLY WHEN HE STICKS HIS NECK OUT.**
9. **THE ELEVATOR AND THE ESCALATOR TO SUCCESS ARE OUT OF ORDER. YOU'LL HAVE TO USE THE STEPS ONE AT A TIME.**
10. **REAL PROS NEVER STOP GOING TO SCHOOL.**

7 RULES FOR SUCCESS

1. **The call you made first is the call you want to make at least.**
2. **Do within forty-eight hours or you probably won't.**
3. **Talk only 30% of the time…You can't learn anything by talking.**
4. **Make three calls by 9 AM every day; you'll increase your business 20%.**
5. **Some will, some won't, so what…NEXT.**
6. **80% of success is showing up!**
7. **Remember, everyone knows 250 people—use your referral tree.**

SUCCESS

A CARNEGIE FOUNDATION STUDY ONCE SHOWED THAT ONLY *15%* OF A BUSINESS PERSON'S SUCCESS COULD BE ATTRIBUTED TO JOB KNOWLEDGE AND TECHNICAL SKILLS….ESSENTIAL ELEMENTS, BUT A SMALL OVERALL CONTRIBUTION.

IT SHOWED THAT *85%* OF ONE'S SUCCESS WOULD BE DETERMINED BY WHAT THEY CALL "ABILITY TO DEAL WITH PEOPLE AND ATTITUDE."

Chapter 10

SUMMARY

REVIEW OF 7- STEP SALES PROCESS

STEP 1: **PAIN**

Remember: NO PAIN…NO CHANGE!

HOW? Ask Questions…

You may have to prompt the pain.

2 PROBLEMS:

- Getting prospect to talk.
- Getting at the real truth.

2 TECHNIQUES:

- Going Left
  Challenging answers and exploring all options that do not involve your product/service (realize that 80% stay with current supplier).
- Client Stories
  "But I am not sure if that applies to you."

STEP 2: INVOLVEMENT

HOW? Simply ask and gain agreement. "Mr. Prospect, now that we've identified some issues, let's work together in designing a unique solution—one that fits your budget or what you are hoping to spend."

2 PROBLEMS:

- Getting prospect to agree.
- Getting prospect to share numbers.

2 TECHNIQUES:

- Walkaway—if he will not get involved—why? Just price shopping?
- Round numbers in the ballpark are OK answers, at least for now.

STEP 3: CUSTOMIZE SOLUTIONS WITHIN BUDGET

Prospect must discover his own solutions.

HOW? Ask how he would like the problem solved?

You may have to "prompt the solution."

1 PROBLEM:

- Getting prospect to discuss the "specifics" of the solution.

1 TECHNIQUE:

- Client stories (suggest two to three options) "But I am not sure any of those would work for you."

As soon as the prospect "Discovers" his own
PAIN and SOLUTIONS …

… What's happening?

The prospect is **selling you** on why he needs your product/service!

Since the prospect is now totally INVOLVED …

It is much easier to

Move to **Step 4!**

STEP 4: **PROSPECT REHEARSAL**

HOW? Tell the stories about two critical statistics and LOYALTY

- 80% stay with the incumbent
- It costs six times as much money to secure a new account than it does to keep an existing one.

1 PROBLEM:

- If the prospect is indeed going to consider a counteroffer, be sure that he does it before you put in a lot of time and effort.

1 TECHNIQUE:

- Going Left…hard! "Mr. Prospect, even if we were to come in with a lower price or lower value, I can't see how you could *ever* refuse their counteroffer, especially when they'll even offer you a credit."

<u>STEP 5:</u> **DECISION PROCESS (REVERSE TIME LINE)**

<u>HOW?</u> Work backwards from delivery/installation date to agreement date (allow for prep time to meet delivery/installation date). Then go to the top of the page—today's date—and begin discussing all steps leading to the agreement/decision date.

<u>1 PROBLEM</u>:

- Getting prospect to live up to the dates.

<u>1 TECHNIQUE:</u>

- Going Left—*stretch* the dates, especially the delivery/installation date to insure the prospect's buy-in (i.e., **his** dates not yours)!

<u>STEP 6</u>: **COMMITMENT**

<u>HOW?</u> Review steps 1, 2, and 3 (which should be the proposal) then "What happens next?"

<u>1 PROBLEM</u>:

- Response is usually…"We'll think about it."

<u>1 TECHNIQUE</u>:

- Plant your feet—"If this were your decision alone, on a scale of 1–10, "10" being "I'd sign now," where are you? Get his buy-in first. Then "Why not run it by your boss. Get his comments first so that we can incorporate them into our final proposal?"

STEP 7: **PROPOSAL: DEVELOPED/WRITTEN TOGETHER**

HOW? Review PAINS, SOLUTIONS, and COSTS with prospect before delivering the proposal.

Never give a proposal to anyone who does not know exactly what's in it.

1 PROBLEM:

- Prospect will not commit and/or has minimal involvement.

2 TECHNIQUES:

- Start over: Go back to the beginning—Step 1, PAIN—"Mr. Prospect, I must have missed something …."

- Two-Sided Proposal

  Left side is your lowest possible price with **no** options.

  Right side lists options; each separately priced with no total number.

MAJOR CONCEPTS

1. Buyers believe that although you may look and act like a nice person, your profession demands that you compromise your ethics and/or integrity.

2. Pain—is the ankle broken or sprained? Test of pain: "On a scale of 1 to 10, "10" being mission critical, you must do it, "1" being it's an irritant but you can live with it. are you?"

3. Going Left—suggest all options that do not include your product/service.

4. Client Stories—tell the story and then add, "But I don't know if this applies to you?"

5. Attempting to become a SALES PSYCHOLOGIST without mastering the two techniques of GOING LEFT and CLIENT STORIES is like trying to play baseball without a bat and ball.

6. Involvement is the key ingredient to a successful sale.

7. The first 5 minutes—conceptually: "Why am I here?"

8. Prospect Rehearsal is the ultimate test of pain, necessitating change vs. just shopping.

9. The Reverse Time Line affords the best opportunity for ferreting out the *real* issues.

10. The only closing question—"What happens next?"

11. When forced to give a proposal (without involvement) make it two-sided.

12. In negotiations, give *only* a little and get something in return.

13. You can't be real and emotional at the same time.

14. Five characteristics of successful salespeople: Connectivity, Intelligence, Self-Confidence, Passion, and Pro-activity (make things happen).

15. Referrals, Referrals, Referrals.

16. We give you the sheet music—you play it (i.e., use these concepts to fit your own personality).

17. We generally work harder to *learn* knowledge than to translate that knowledge into *skills.*

PRACTICE, PRACTICE, PRACTICE!

SALES QUESTIONAIRE

1. #1 Sales Rule: NO _________, NO ____________.
2. What percentage of people/organizations keep their current vendor even when they are SLIGHTLY unhappy? ____%
3. How much more money does it cost to keep an existing client vs. finding a new one? $ ______
4. With the above two points in mind, what happens in most "BID" situations? ____

   ____

   ____
5. When does the prospect find out whose product/service is better?

   ____

   ____
6. Therefore, a "safe" decision for most prospects is a decision based primarily on ____
7. Beside price, why else will prospects change vendors?

   ____
8. What is the best/quickest way to develop "trust"? _______________
9. Are people more likely to accept an idea they perceive as their own or an idea they perceive as someone else's? ___________________

   ____
10. What then can be the real "differentiator" between you and your competitors? ____

    ____
11. ___% of the time prospects pains are serious enough for them to make a change?

12. In a prospect situation requiring a bid with minimum information provided and little if any contact—what % do you win? Be honest! _____%

13. Is there any value in giving a proposal in the above situation? Any negatives? ____
____

14. How will you respond to the prospect who only wants your solution/price and NO involvement? ___________________________
____

Answers are on the next page.

ANSWERS TO SALES QUESTIONAIRE

1. Pain, Change
2. 80%
3. 6 times as much
4. Price shopping—if a lower bid is received, the company will ask/demand that the current vendor match it.
5. AFTER the agreement is signed
6. Price
7. Belief and **trust** that the new product/service is superior
8. Going Left—suggesting options that do not involve your product/service
9. Their own
10. The sales process—total INVOLVEMENT
11. 20%
12. General population—2%
13. Positive: Prospect gets to know you for possible future sale Negative: If you are higher priced, you will get the reputation for being high and will always be asked to bid when the prospect wants to protect his incumbent.
14. Walkaway power: "Mr. Prospect, put yourself in my place. If you knew in your heart of hearts that a process you were about to enter into was not in your own best interest, but even more importantly it was not in your prospect's best interest, what would **you** do?"

SALES PSYCHOLOGY RULES

1. NO PAIN, NO CHANGE.
2. Get REAL—say or ask what you feel.
    a. 65% of prospects that salespeople work on at any given time NEVER result in a sale.
    b. 80% of prospects stay with their current suppliers even when slightly unhappy.
    c. It costs six times as much to secure a new client than it does to keep an existing one.
    d. You can't be real and emotional at the same time.
3. BE THE WINNER OR THE FIRST ONE OUT.
4. OUR JOB IS TO GET A DECISION—"No" and "No for now" are decisions.
    a. You don't learn how to win by getting a "Yes"—you learn by getting a "No."
5. YOU CAN'T SELL ANYONE ANYTHING—THEY MUST DISCOVER THEY WANT IT!
6. NO GUESSING—only encourages others to consider you "ignorant" or "arrogant."
7. ASK TOUGH QUESTIONS—THEY ACTUALLY HELP BUILD RAPPORT.
    a. Before asking a tough question—softening statement (i.e., "Don't get me wrong, I want this business…").
8. DEVELOP WALKAWAY POWER.
9. NO RISK, NO NOTHING! Take more chances than you dare.
10. NEVER GIVE A PROPSAL TO ONE WHO DOES NOT KNOW EXACTLY WHAT'S IN IT.
11. Whenever you offer a prospect a solution, you are actually encouraging him/her to shop you—better solution and/or better price.
12. Never defend your price—you can't.
13. Never be the first one to offer the exact number.
14. Never lead with a lower price. Someone will always match it or even beat it.

15. If you have to give something, get something in return.
16. Prospects feel that although you may look and act like a nice person, your profession demands that you compromise your ethics and/or integrity.
17. I've got a problem, I need your help…
18. People buy EMOTIONALLY; they reinforce their decisions INTELLECTUALLY.
19. Prepare for appointments with the attitude: I'm going to make the PROSPECT SELL ME on why he/she wants my product/service.
20. Close the file for now.
21. Conversation, not presentation. Become a facilitator rather than a presenter.
22. Plan your day the night before, including the specific times for each item, allowing time for interruptions.
23. Execute your plan; only allow for real—not perceived priorities.
24. Following a meeting or seminar, plan a course of action within forty-eight hours or you probably won't.
25. As you get comfortable with this new selling process, put the "concepts" into your own words.

Chapter 11

GETTING STARTED

**"IF I HAD 8 HOURS TO CHOP DOWN A TREE,
I WOULD SPEND 6 HOURS SHARPENING MY AX."**

— Abraham Lincoln

As we begin to change our behavior and learn new skills, keep in mind that no book on selling will in itself improve your selling skills any more than reading a book about swimming will make you a swimmer. How many nonswimmers would jump in the ocean immediately after reading such a book?

Also, keep in mind that it is more important to project one's personality into a discussion rather than taking our suggestions **too** literally. Remember the old adage: *"It's not what you say, but how you say it."*

On the other hand, don't struggle too long before using the new concepts. "Fail my way first." By this we mean that your initial responses may not be just right, so don't be afraid to use our verbiage in the beginning.

Neil Rackham states: "success in any skill—golf, piano, selling—rests on concentrated tedious and frustrating practice." **The sad fact is we generally work harder to *learn* knowledge than to translate that knowledge into *skills*.** For example, in a recent study of 200 golfers who took lessons, 157 played worse immediately following the lessons.

Some notes when learning new skills:

1. Practice only one behavior at a time.

2. New skills take time to become *instinctive.* Expect several failures. Remember, we learn more from failures than successes.

3. Concentrate on using a lot of the behavior rather than using it well…quantity before quality.

4. Practice in safe situations, particularly when first learning a new skill.

You've heard it before, "The most difficult step is the first one." Once you're committed to becoming a sales psychologist, the first step is *Practice, Practice, Practice!*

However, we believe in preparation. The proven most effective process is as follows:

1. Make good use of a voice recorder.

2. Write out the actual subject matter you decide to work on (e.g., The first 5 minutes—"why am I here?") Better yet, use the quotes from this book. I know, they're not your words; nevertheless, don't get creative initially—learn the fundamentals first.

3. Use your driving time to listen to your recording.

4. Gradually, record yourself without the script. Keep recording over and over until it sounds just like you want. Do not be surprised if it takes a while.

Note: When you do this last step, you'll appreciate that you didn't start with live prospects.

5. Follow this procedure for any and all new information.

6. Now, practice on anyone who will listen to you.

Our own experience has shown that only about 10% of people are committed enough to follow the above. Are you in that 10%?

Note: The post call checklist is provided to act as a reminder/review for each of your calls.

POST CALL CHECKLIST

Before you leave the prospect's parking lot, ask yourself these questions:

1. What are the pain issues – serious enough to change?

2. Did all participants understand Involvement? More importantly, did they agree to working together? If not, why not? If yes, how do I know?

3. If it's a bid situation, will they work with us, i.e. can we help write the specs; will they share approximate numbers?

4. Did the prospect discover H/H own solutions? Or... Did we give options that other clients have used?

5. What's the prospect hoping to spend?

6. Have we agreed on a planning process – Reverse Timeline?

7. Do we have an agreed-upon next step – date and agenda?

8. Do we have a commitment before proposal –
   "What Happens Next?"

9. What's the one tough question I should have asked?

10. What's the one thing that could kill this deal?

11. Did I become emotional or did I stay in the sales process?

The difference between extraordinary people and ordinary people is as simple as the difference between the two words.

Extraordinary people are committed to doing the extra things that ordinary people won't.

— Christine Kinney

If a man does his best what else is there?

— George Patton

GOOD LUCK

ENJOY THE JOURNEY!

75120734R00120

Made in the USA
Columbia, SC
17 August 2017